AS/A-LEVEL

STUDENT GUIDE

AQA

Geography

Component 2:
Human geography

Global systems
Global governance
Changing places

David Redfern

HODDER
EDUCATION
AN HACHETTE UK COMPANY

Hodder Education, an Hachette UK company, Blenheim Court, George Street, Banbury, Oxfordshire OX16 5BH

Orders

Bookpoint Ltd, 130 Park Drive, Milton Park, Abingdon, Oxfordshire OX14 4SB

tel: 01235 827827

fax: 01235 400401

e-mail: education@bookpoint.co.uk

Lines are open 9.00 a.m.–5.00 p.m., Monday to Saturday, with a 24-hour message answering service. You can also order through the Hodder Education website: www.hoddereducation.co.uk

This Guide has been written specifically to support students preparing for the AQA AS and A-level Geography examinations. The content has been neither approved nor endorsed by AQA and remains the sole responsibility of the author.

Cover photo: pure-life-pictures/Fotolia; photos on page 54: Yvonne Follows-Smith and David Redfern

Typeset by Integra Software Services Pvt. Ltd., Pondicherry, India

Printed in Italy

Hachette UK's policy is to use papers that are natural, renewable and recyclable products and made from wood grown in sustainable forests. The logging and manufacturing processes are expected to conform to the environmental regulations of the country of origin.

Contents

Content Guidance

Questions & Answers

■ Getting the most from this book

Exam-style questions

Commentary on the questions

Tips on what you need to do to gain full marks, indicated by the icon **e**.

Sample student answers

Practise the questions, then look at the student answers that follow.

Commentary on sample student answers

Read the comments (preceded by the icon **e**) showing how many marks each answer would be awarded in the exam and exactly where marks are gained or lost.

Set of questions B

Question 1

Describe the physical geography of Antarctica.   (4 marks)

e Mark scheme: 1 mark per valid point.

Student A

Antarctica is 14 million km² in size **a** and 98% of its surface area consists of ice that averages 2km in thickness. **b** In terms of climate, it is a cold desert with an annual precipitation of only 200mm along the coast, **c** and with lower totals inland. Around the coasts, temperatures are generally close to freezing in the summer months, or even slightly positive in the northern part of the Antarctic Peninsula. **d** During winter, monthly mean temperatures at coastal stations are between −10°C and −30°C, but temperatures may briefly rise towards freezing when winter storms bring warm air towards the Antarctic coast. **e**

e 4/4 marks awarded. **a**–**e** Student A provides several valid descriptive statements.

Student B

Antarctica, the southernmost continent and site of the South Pole, is a virtually uninhabited, ice-covered land mass. **a** Most cruises to the continent visit the Antarctic Peninsula, which stretches toward South America. The cold continent's isolated landscape shelters rich wildlife, including many penguins. **b**

e 1/4 marks awarded. **a** It is difficult to find any statement of A-level quality, but perhaps 1 mark could be awarded for two weak descriptions.

Question 2

Table 2 shows information relating to internet usage around the world by region. Interpret the information shown.   (6 marks)

Table 2 World internet usage by region (2014)

World region	Population (millions)	% of population with access to the internet	Growth of internet usage 2000–14 (%)	Proportion of world users of the internet (%)
Africa	1,136	26.5	6,499	9.8
Asia	4,096	34.7	1,113	45.7
Europe	741	70.5	454	19.2
Middle East	255	48.3	3,304	3.7
North America	353	87.7	187	10.2
Latin America	618	52.3	1,673	10.5
Oceania	39	72.9	252	0.9
World	7,238	42.3	741	100

Source: www.internetworldstats.com/stats.htm

■ About this book

Much of the knowledge and understanding needed for AS and A-level geography builds on what you have learned for GCSE geography, but with an added focus on key geographical concepts and depth of knowledge and understanding of content. This guide offers advice for the effective revision of **Human geography**, which all students need to complete.

In the A-level Paper 2 external exam, Section A tests your knowledge and application of aspects of Global systems and global governance, and Section B tests Changing places. (The content for Section C is not covered in this guide.) The whole exam lasts 2 hours and 30 minutes, and the unit makes up 40% of the A-level award. The topic Changing places also makes up 50% of the AS Paper 2, which lasts a total of 1 hour and 30 minutes. More information on the exam papers is given in the Questions & Answers section (pages 47–83).

To be successful in this unit you have to understand:

■ the key ideas of the content
■ the nature of the assessment material — by reviewing and practising sample structured questions
■ how to achieve a high level of performance within them.

This guide has two sections:

Content Guidance — this summarises some of the key information that you need to know to be able to answer the examination questions with a high degree of accuracy and depth. In particular, the meaning of keys terms is made clear and some attention is paid to providing details of case study material to help to meet the spatial context requirement within the specification.

Questions & Answers — this includes some sample questions similar in style to those you might expect in the exam. There are some sample student responses to these questions as well as detailed analysis, which will give further guidance in relation to what exam markers are looking for to award top marks.

The best way to use this book is to read through the relevant topic area first before practising the questions. Only refer to the answers and examiner comments after you have attempted the questions.

Content Guidance

This section outlines the following areas of the AQA AS and A-level Geography specifications:

■ Global systems and global governance (A-level only)
■ Changing places (AS and A-level)

Read through the chosen topic area(s) before attempting questions from the Questions & Answers section.

■ Global systems

Globalisation

Dimensions and factors of globalisation

Globalisation has a range of meanings. The way it is defined in any context tends to reflect the priorities or prejudices of whoever is writing. Economists, historians and geographers may all define globalisation differently, according to their own interests. Some people may take a scientific viewpoint and define globalisation in a way that is free of any values or perspectives. Others believe that the impact of globalisation on people's lives means there should always be a moral or ethical dimension to its discussion.

Geographers describe globalisation in general terms as the process by which places and environments become more:

■ **interconnected**
■ **interdependent**
■ **deeply connected**
■ connected together in real-time as part of a **shrinking world** (also known as **time/ space compression**)

This 'shrinking world' concept has been enhanced by the use of information and communications technology (ICT). An important outcome of the relationship between ICT and globalisation is the growth of extensive networks of people and places. All kinds of global networks can be modelled, ranging from social networks such as Facebook and Twitter to the complex supply chains of global corporations.

ICT enables all these interactions by providing affordable, instantaneous connectivity. Over time, network connections have become faster and more inclusive of all people in society, not just privileged groups. As a result, a staggering amount of globally available digital information has been created since 2000.

Globalisation The growing economic interdependence of countries worldwide through increasing volume and variety of cross-border transactions in goods and services, freer international flows of capital and labour, and more rapid and widespread diffusion of technology.

Knowledge check 1

Illustrate some aspects of the 'shrinking world'.

Exam tip

The use of the internet and its impact on globalisation is changing all the time. Be prepared to be very topical in this area.

Types of globalisation

Economic globalisation

The growth of transnational corporations (TNCs) has accelerated cross-border exchanges of raw materials, components, finished manufactured goods, shares, portfolio investment and purchasing. ICT supports the growth of complex spatial divisions of labour for firms and a more international economy. The internet and World Wide Web have allowed extensive networks of consumption to develop (such as online purchasing on eBay and Amazon).

Political globalisation

The growth of trading blocs (e.g. the European Union (EU), the North American Free Trade Association (NAFTA)) allows TNCs to merge and make acquisitions of firms in neighbouring countries, while reduced trade restrictions and tariffs help markets to grow.

The G7/G8 and G20 groups of countries meet regularly to discuss global concerns such as the global economy and the environment (the financial crash of 2007 and climate change being two major issues of recent years). The World Bank, the International Monetary Fund (IMF) and the World Trade Organization (WTO) work internationally to harmonise national economies.

Social globalisation

International migration has created extensive family networks that cross national borders. City societies across the globe have become multi-ethnic and pluralistic. Global improvements in education and health can be seen over time, with rising life expectancy and literacy levels, although the changes are by no means uniform or universal. Social interconnectivity has grown over time due to the spread of universal connections such as mobile phones, email and the use of 'social media'.

Cultural globalisation

Successful Western cultural traits have come to dominate in some nations — sometimes called the Americanisation or 'McDonaldisation' of tastes and fashions. 'Glocalisation' is a more complex outcome that takes place as old local cultures merge and meld with globalising influences. The circulation of ideas and information has accelerated due to 24-hour news reporting; people also keep in touch using virtual spaces such as Facebook, Skype, Twitter and WhatsApp. The latter have been linked to the globalisation of terrorism.

A final way of considering globalisation is to describe it as the latest chapter in a long story of global trade, migration and cultural change. Globalisation can be said to be the continuation of a far older, and ongoing, economic and political project of empire-building. Globalisation can therefore be seen as a series of periods in an economic, social, political and cultural story:

- **Period 1 During the 1950s:** the end of the age of colonial empires with, for example, independence for African and Asian countries; post-war settlements and bodies (the IMF, World Bank, General Agreement on Tariffs and Trade (GATT) and the WTO); the growth of container shipping.

- **Period 2 Between the 1960s and the 1980s:** the rise of the Asian Tigers (Hong Kong, South Korea, Taiwan, Singapore) and deindustrialisation of parts of Western core countries; the rising influence of the Organization of Petroleum Exporting Countries (OPEC) and their oil price rises; offshoring beginning in earnest; the spread of financial deregulation and the growth of money markets.
- **Period 3 The 1990s to the present day:** the fall of the Soviet Union; the growth of the BRIC (Brazil, Russia, India, China) economies; the growth of trade blocs (EU, NAFTA); the acceleration of technology; punctuated by periods of economic crisis.
- **Period 4 The future:** the rise and rise of China and India and some new emerging economies such as Indonesia and Malaysia.

Knowledge check 2

In addition to the BRIC countries, geographers now refer to the MINT countries. Name them.

Global marketing

When a company decides to embark on **global marketing**, it views the world as one market and creates products that fit the various regional marketplaces. The ultimate goal is to sell the same thing, the same way, everywhere. Some examples include:

- **Coca-Cola:** the company uses the same formulae (one with sugar, the other with corn syrup) for all its markets. The classic contour bottle design is incorporated in every country, although the size of bottle and can that is marketed is the same size as other beverage bottles and cans in any particular country.
- **Mars:** the company introduced a chocolate bar called 'Snickers' around the world, though for a time, until 1990, it was marketed under the name 'Marathon' in the UK and Ireland.
- **Lever Brothers:** in 2000, Lever Brothers (UK) decided to rename its household cleaning product 'Jif' to 'Cif', the company's global moniker for the product.

In many cases it seems that the common factor is the need to align with markets in the USA and far east.

Global marketing
Marketing on a worldwide scale, reconciling or taking commercial advantage of global operational differences, similarities and opportunities in order to meet global objectives.

Exam tip

What other products have you seen on your holidays that are the same or similar to those in your country?

Global patterns of production, distribution and consumption

Globalisation has brought about a new international division of labour. At its simplest, it is possible to recognise two groups:

- Occupations that are highly skilled, highly paid and involve research and development (R&D), decision-making and managerial roles. These are largely concentrated in developed (or high-income) countries.
- Occupations that are unskilled and poorly paid assembly roles. These tend to be located in the emerging economies, often developing (or low-income) countries, based on low labour costs.

This simple division has undergone radical changes in the last 50 years. Many countries that were classified as developing have become newly industrialised countries (NICs) and even within this group it is possible to recognise several generations, all at various stages of development.

In the mid-1950s, around 95% of manufacturing was concentrated in the industrialised economies. Since then, decentralisation has occurred, which has been largely the result of **foreign direct investment** by TNCs in those developing

Foreign direct investment (FDI) The money invested into a country by TNCs or other national governments.

countries able to take on manufacturing tasks at a competitive price. This filtering down of manufacturing industry from developed countries to lower-wage economies has become known as a 'global shift'. It has also resulted from the fact that high technology is no longer associated with high productivity and high wages.

The **transfer of technology** enables many countries within the developing world to increase their productivity without raising their wages to the levels of developed countries. This could also widen the development gap, as workers in the developing world are paid less to make the same products as their counterparts in developed countries. By the first decade of the twenty-first century, over 50% of all manufacturing jobs were located in the developing world and over 60% of exports from such countries to the developed world were of manufactured goods.

The provision of services has become increasingly detached from that of the production of goods. The financial sector, for example, has no direct relationship to manufacturing. Therefore, as manufacturing has become dispersed world wide, high-level services have increasingly concentrated in places different from the old centres of manufacturing.

The 1990s, however, saw the emergence of a growing number of transnational service conglomerates, seeking to extend their influence on a global scale, particularly in banking and other financial services, and advertising. The movement of capital around the world has speeded up, with the outcome that conglomerates now own many manufacturing and service industries, purely for their financial gain. Such organisations are known as private equity firms and venture capitalists.

Another recent trend has been the decentralisation of low-level services from the developed to the developing world. Call centre operations, for example, have moved from the UK to India, the middle east and South Africa, where employment costs are generally at least 10–20% lower. This globalisation of services is simply following what has been happening in manufacturing over several decades.

One of the consequences of a global shift in the developed world has been deindustrialisation. This has not been entirely due to a global shift, as other factors such as outmoded production methods, long-established products entering the end of their life cycles and poor management have all contributed to the decline in manufacturing in those regions.

Global systems

This section examines the form and nature of the interdependencies and interconnections (economic, political, social and environmental) in the world today.

Globalisation and global systems have created a number of issues including:
- unequal flows of people, money, ideas and technology, which in some cases can act to promote stability, economic growth and development but can also cause further inequalities, conflicts and injustices for people and the places in which they live
- unequal power relations that enable some nations to drive global systems to their own advantage and directly influence geopolitical events, while other nations are only able to respond or resist in a more constrained way

Transfer of technology
The movement of ideas and technology from one region or country to another.

Knowledge check 3

Where are the major financial services located in the world today?

These are very complex issues, with a recurrent theme of inequality. This theme can be considered in terms of the benefits and the costs of globalisation, followed by an examination of some of the effects that it has produced.

Benefits of globalisation

The benefits of globalisation depend on the perspective of the person seeking benefit. It is clear that the growing interdependence of nations largely through the activities of TNCs has brought benefits to both the host countries and the countries of origin involved.

In general terms, for the host country:

- TNCs are a vital source of FDI — globalisation has created jobs all over the world.
- TNCs stimulate the multiplier effect, locally and nationally. The company itself may require locally produced components and other supply and distribution services. Meanwhile, increased wealth and disposable incomes will generate domestic demand and stimulate further growth. At a national level, revenues become available for investment in social forms of development — in public services such as health and education.
- TNCs not only provide employment, they also increase local skills. In some cases, this may help to offset large-scale unemployment caused by the mechanisation of agriculture.
- TNCs are often responsible for the transfer of technology such as 'just-in-time' (JIT) production (see page 21).
- TNCs may construct or improve local infrastructure such as roads, bridges, etc., which benefits not only the company but the local area overall.

Still in the context of host countries, it is sometimes stated that globalisation has brought stability to the world, perhaps not economically as seen by the recession that took place during and since 2007/8, but politically. It is suggested that countries that depend upon each other economically are unlikely to be at odds with each other, certainly not in a military context. Whether or not countries are friendlier towards each other, it seems to be the case that the world appears to have a greater degree of political stability. That said, another country reaping the benefits of globalisation is Russia, and yet it seems to want to spread its political influence once again, thereby creating some sense of instability around the world.

Although it is common for TNCs to move production to overseas locations, the headquarters usually remain in the company's country of origin. Other high-salary jobs stay, such as those in R&D, further enhancing skills levels. TNCs that move to locations with cheaper labour usually increase their profitability, which benefits the country of origin, as profits are returned for distribution to shareholders. Even the largest TNCs retain a physical foothold in the countries in which they are domiciled. This provides them with a sense of national identity. The national government of the country where a TNC is domiciled will benefit, as it collects corporation tax on its profits.

Multiplier effect A form of positive feedback where an initial investment creates more investment, both social and economic.

Knowledge check 4

What is 'just-in-time' production?

Exam tip

Monitor recent events to track the growing influence of countries such as Russia and China in the world.

Costs of globalisation

As well as benefits, there have been significant costs of globalisation, particularly in terms of the effects on people, local economies, cultures and the environment. They have often led to disagreements, conflicts, instability and injustices.

In general terms, the costs of globalisation are as follows:

■ TNCs can prove lethal competition for local firms, which may go out of business, creating hostility among local people.

■ TNCs often face negative attitudes from local authorities, residents and environmentalists.

■ Many of the jobs offered are low skilled. Managerial positions are often filled by people who have moved with the TNC, providing little prospect for locals to develop within their jobs and gain promotion.

■ Some TNCs stand accused of exploiting cheap, flexible, non-unionised labour in sweatshops in developing countries. Working conditions in some factories are harsh: long hours for very little pay and employees get few work-related benefits.

■ TNCs can be fickle employers, moving elsewhere in the interests of profitability with little concern for locals. Branch plants can often be the first to close, or be subject to merger, causing job losses.

■ Much of the capital generated finds its way back to the country of origin.

Globalisation also results in TNCs being vulnerable to risks often beyond their control, some natural and some human. Exposure to risks and to more volatile market forces in an interconnected and interdependent world is a big concern for major companies.

Impacts of globalisation

It is often stated that TNCs exploit cheap, flexible, non-unionised labour forces in the developing world. It is true that in the last two decades there has been considerable use of **outsourcing** and **offshoring** strategies. It is equally true that most large TNCs have established a basic standard of operation, which involves setting up training facilities for workers and providing promotion opportunities for host country employees, and minimum wage and safety limits.

TNCs have moved to developing countries in order to make use of their labour supplies created by the so-called **demographic dividend**. A demographic dividend occurs when the population of working age in a country is large in relation to the population of non-working age. High rates of economic growth led by high productivity and supported by large working populations create the 'dividend'. There have also been movements of people around the world to find employment where it is available. In most cases labour migrants are in search of work and better-paid jobs so that they can send money back to their families as remittances. This phenomenon is called the international movement of labour.

Exam tip

One of the best-documented examples of outsourcing and offshoring is that of the TNC Apple in China, at locations such as Foxconn City. You could investigate it.

Exam tip

Research the impact of natural events (such as the Tohoku tsunami, 2011) and human events (such as the Deepwater Horizon disaster, 2010) on TNCs.

Outsourcing When a TNC subcontracts an 'overseas' company to produce goods or services on its behalf.

Offshoring The manufacture or assembly of a product in a developing country using components produced in a developed country.

Demographic dividend Occurs when there are fewer dependent children and elderly with relatively more productive adults in a population.

It is suggested that you now examine a number of **case studies**, such as Foxconn City, of the impacts of specific TNCs and/or activities in a variety of locations around the world. Select a range of contexts and a range of impacts, some positive and some negative.

Unequal power relations

Unequal power relations at a national scale can be discussed in the context of China and its relations with the rest of the world. At the end of the 1970s, Deng Xiaoping's China began to 'open its doors' to the rest of the world, turning its back on the period under Chairman Mao. Xiaoping recognised that if China as a whole was to become prosperous, some regions would have to become rich before others. He allowed the coastal regions to develop at a much faster pace than the inland regions, even if inequality occurred as a result. The liberalisation of trade through joining the World Trade Organization (WTO) in 2001 has also helped greatly.

A key aspect of China's growth has been the setting up of Special Economic Zones (SEZs) along the east coast. These are designated areas of very fast economic development. They have special regulations and fewer restrictions on growth, while also offering higher wages than in the rest of China. China's eastern region contains its top three municipalities — Beijing, Shanghai and Tianjin. It also includes the country's largest city economies of Guangdong Province (including Guangzhou and Shenzen), Shenyang and Hangzhou. Guangdong Province alone has the same population as Mexico and if it was an independent country it would have the 17th largest GDP in the world. It accounts for 25% of China's international trade and has become a magnet for migrant workers from across the country. Its growth and economic development have been huge. However, there has been an associated increase in income inequality within the country.

In terms of industry, the state-owned enterprises (SOEs) were reformed. A key incentive was to allow them to keep some of their profits for further investment. In addition, they improved their management strategies, and some smaller SOEs were privatised. On a general level there have been fewer barriers to collaboration with foreign partners, and hence several SOEs have attracted foreign TNCs as partners and FDI has been significant, as have joint ventures (JVs). There has also been more westernisation in terms of profit-and-loss accounting, patent legislation, and scientific and technological research. Competition is now encouraged. Some major Chinese companies that have set up JVs with other foreign companies include Sinopec, PetroChina, China Mobile and Shanghai Automotive Industry Corps (SAIC).

There were other benefits from China's growth. Infrastructural improvements — ports, railways, roads, airports — built initially for industrial and trade purposes are also available for other forms of international travel or trade. They allow China to integrate more with the world and they are also a catalyst for rapidly rising living standards. It is not just the case that China can export more; it can also import more, increasing its dependence on other countries for the goods and services that the rising number of middle classes desire.

Exam tip

Use an atlas to locate these cities and areas.

Knowledge check 5

Summarise the main causes of economic growth in India.

Who are China's rivals?

For some time now, Brazil, Russia, India, China and South Africa have been grouped together under the acronym BRICS. The BRICS' gross domestic product (GDP) totalled US$16 trillion in 2012. This compares with US$17 trillion for the EU and US$16 trillion for the USA. However China alone accounts for 55% of the BRICS' GDP; take China out, and they are much less powerful economically.

We must also note that there are other 'kids on the bloc' such as Mexico, Nigeria, Bangladesh, Vietnam, South Korea, Indonesia, Turkey and Egypt. Many of these emerging nations share the characteristic of the demographic dividend. They have youthful populations today, but fertility levels are falling. They have a window of opportunity when their workforce is large, but does not have to support either a large young or old population.

China: going global?

China is expanding into the rest of the world. It has over US$1.2 trillion to invest overseas. China also owns US$1.3 trillion of US debt. So where is this investment going?

- USA: into the energy sector and finance industries
- Brazil: into development of its natural resources, both agricultural and mineral
- Australia: into the resources of iron ore, coal and gas
- Nigeria: investment in oil, mostly through engineering and construction
- UK: buying on the property market and in shares on the London Stock Exchange
- Saudi Arabia: currently linked to infrastructural construction
- Iran: infrastructural construction and energy related

China is also investing heavily in sub-Saharan Africa, often in infrastructure projects. Furthermore, over 1 million Chinese live in Africa, some for the long term or even permanently, having bought land and started businesses. Chinese trade with Africa is currently US$200 billion a year, and most of this is in the export of oil and minerals from Africa to China.

Examples of Chinese investment include the following:

- In Angola, China has helped to reconstruct the country after its long civil war. Loans, secured by access to Angolan oil reserves, have been used to build roads, railways, water systems, hospitals and schools.
- Nigeria took out similar oil-backed loans to finance gas-fired electricity generating stations.
- Chinese technicians have built an HEP plant in the Congo (to be repaid in oil) and another in Ghana (to be paid for with cocoa beans).

Exam tip

China is also investing in the Pacific area. Investigate some of its activities in islands such as Fiji, Samoa and Vanuatu.

International trade and access to markets

The basis of the **trade** of goods and services can be explained by the theory of **comparative advantage**; countries specialise in activities for which they are best equipped in terms of resources and technology. A country can then trade surpluses in order to provide the income needed to buy in goods that cannot be produced efficiently, or at all, in the home economy.

When studying these topics, you should consider how international trade and variable access to markets underlies and impacts on people's lives across the globe. In addition, you should consider how they impact on your life, and influence the way in which you live.

Global features and trends

Data on international trade are extensive, so it is easier to try and condense them into a series of statements and a table (Table 1). In 2013:

- The top ten trading nations accounted for 52% of global trade in goods. Developing countries accounted for 44%. The total value of exports of goods was US$17.8 trillion.
- The top ten trading nations accounted for 50% of global trade in commercial services. Developing countries accounted for 34%. The total value of exports of services was US$4.6 trillion.
- 52% of exports of goods from developing economies are sent to other developing economies. On the other hand, developed countries sent 30% of their exports to developing countries.
- Trade with least developed countries (LDCs) by both developed and developing countries is increasing, but they are both small in amount.
- LDC exports amounted to US$215 billion. 44% of this was exported to Asia (23% to China), 24% to Europe (20% to the EU) and 12% to North America.
- China became the world's biggest trader in goods, with imports and exports totalling US$4,159 billion. It recorded a trade surplus of US$259 billion.
- The USA was the second-biggest trader in goods, with imports and exports totalling US$3,909 billion. The US trade deficit was US$750 billion. Germany was in third place, with a trade surplus of US$264 billion.
- World exports of commercial services totalled US$4,645 billion. The regional share in world exports of commercial services has changed in recent years. In 2013, Europe's exports of commercial services accounted for 47% of world receipts, down from 52% in 2005. There were rising exports by other regions, such as Asia, which accounted for 26% of global services exports in 2013. This was driven by increasing commercial services in India, Macao and Thailand.

Exam tip

There are a lot of figures in this section. You should try to remember some of the key figures and proportions.

Trade The movement of goods and services from producers to consumers. In geographical terms it is measured by movement of these items from one country to another.

Comparative advantage The principle that countries can benefit from specialising in the production of goods at which they are relatively more efficient or skilled.

Table 1 Exports and imports for a selected group of countries (2013)

Rank	Exporter	Value (US$bn)	Share (%)	Rank	Importer	Value (US$bn)	Share (%)
1	China	2,209	11.7	1	USA	2,329	12.3
2	USA	1,580	8.4	2	China	1,950	10.3
3	Germany	1,453	7.7	3	Germany	1,189	6.3
4	Japan	715	3.8	4	Japan	833	4.4
8	UK	542	2.9	6	UK	655	3.5
10	Russia	523	2.8	12	India	466	2.5
19	India	313	1.7	16	Russia	343	1.8
22	Brazil	242	1.3	22	Brazil	250	1.3

Source: WTO (2014)

Trends in foreign investment

A report by the UN Conference on Trade and Development (UNCTAD) in 2014 showed that inflows of global foreign direct investment (FDI) grew to US$1.45tn in 2013. It expected that to rise to US$1.85tn in 2016. Flows to developing countries reached a record high of US$778bn, which makes them worth 54% of the worldwide amount. This meant that developing countries took more investment than developed ones, which, with US$566bn, had a historically low share of 39%.

FDI to the EU began to grow again, with its member countries receiving US$246bn, an increase of 14% on 2012. However, the EU still received less than 30% of what it was getting in its peak year 2007. Although Latin America and the Caribbean saw overall positive growth in FDI inflows, it was mostly due to growth in central America, despite an overall 6% decline in South America. Table 2 shows the top ten host countries for FDI in 2013. The USA stays as the top country, with US$188 billion investment after growth of 17%.

Table 2 Top ten host countries for FDI inflows (2013) US$ millions

Rank	Country	Amount of FDI (US$m)	% change from 2012
1	USA	187,528	17
2	China	123,911	2
3	Russia	79,262	57
4	Hong Kong	64,045	2
5	Brazil	63,772	-2
6	Singapore	62,325	4
7	Canada	49,826	45
8	Australia	39,167	-10
9	Spain	38,286	52
10	Mexico	37,101	117

Source: UNCTAD 2014

> **Exam tip**
>
> Develop the technique of examining sets of data such as those shown in Table 2. Think about relative amounts, and directions and rates of change. Note, for example, that FDI into Mexico doubled in 1 year.

The report also looked at the amount spent by companies and other bodies in each country. These are called FDI outflows. Despite a decline of 14.5%, North America (USA and Canada) is the top region of outward investment of US$381 billion. Outward investment from Asia is increasing — FDI outflows from China grew to US$101 billion in 2013 and are expected to surpass its inflows within 3 years.

Trading relationships and patterns

Trading relations and patterns have been determined over the last 70 years by a series of trade agreements and principles, which have been established to deal with the rapid rise of international trade and the issues associated with it. They deal with trade between the large developed economies (e.g. the USA and the EU), emerging economies (e.g. China and India) and smaller, less developed economies, such as in Latin America and southern Asia. These agreements and principles can be examined at the international and regional scale.

The World Trade Organization

The **World Trade Organization (WTO)** replaced the General Agreement on Tariffs and Trade (GATT) in 1995. It deals with the global rules of trade between nations. Its main function is to ensure that trade flows as smoothly, predictably and freely as possible. At its heart are the WTO agreements, negotiated and signed by the bulk of the world's trading nations and ratified in their parliaments. Where countries have faced trade barriers and wanted them lowered, WTO-led negotiations have helped to open markets for trade.

WTO agreements contain special provision for developing countries, including longer time periods to implement agreements and commitments, measures to increase their trading opportunities, and support to help them build their trade capacity.

The European Union

The **European Union (EU)** was known as the European Community prior to 1 November 1993 and before that as the European Economic Community. It currently consists of 28 members: France, Germany, the Netherlands, Belgium, Luxembourg, Italy (the first six members), the UK, Denmark, Ireland (joined 1973), Greece (1981), Portugal and Spain (1986), Austria, Finland and Sweden (1995), Czech Republic, Cyprus, Estonia, Hungary, Latvia, Lithuania, Malta, Poland, Slovakia and Slovenia (2004), Romania and Bulgaria (2007), and Croatia (2013).

The EU was established under the Treaty of Rome in 1957 with the objective of removing all trade barriers between member states. The background to this was the desire to form a political and economic union that would prevent the possibility of another war in Europe.

The majority of the countries in the EU use a single currency: the euro. The Treaty of Maastricht (1991) paved the way for monetary union, which came about in 2002 with the adoption of the euro. Some countries — the UK, Denmark and Sweden — do not take part in this zone. Since then, Cyprus, Malta and Slovenia have been accepted into the Eurozone and it is hoped that all the nations that joined the EU in 2004 and 2007 will eventually adopt the euro. Slovakia joined the Eurozone in 2009. In the UK there has been an ongoing debate regarding the merits or otherwise of the EU. This culminated in June 2016 with a referendum result calling for the UK to leave the EU.

Knowledge check 6

Assemble three arguments for and three arguments against a country staying within the EU.

The North American Free Trade Area

The **North American Free Trade Area**'s (**NAFTA**) members consist of the USA, Canada and Mexico in an attempt to create the equivalent of the single European market within the North American continent. Its biggest geographical impact has been to create the maquiladora in Mexico. These are manufacturing industries operating in a Mexican free trade zone close to the USA–Mexico border, where factories import material and equipment on a duty-free and tariff-free basis for assembly, processing or manufacturing. The products are then re-exported back to the USA and Canada. This is offshoring on a huge scale, based entirely on numerous low-cost labour forces in northern Mexico.

The Association of Southeast Asian Nations

The **Association of Southeast Asian Nations (ASEAN)** is a political and economic organisation of ten southeast Asian countries. It was formed in 1967 by Indonesia, Malaysia, the Philippines, Singapore and Thailand. Since then membership has expanded to include Brunei, Cambodia, Laos, Myanmar (Burma) and Vietnam. Its aims include accelerating economic growth and social progress among its members, protection of regional peace and stability, and opportunities for member countries to resolve differences peacefully.

Changes in global trade patterns

Huge changes are taking place in the pattern of trade around the world. Trade involving the emerging economies has been growing rapidly, so much so that for many such nations trade with other countries in the emerging world is now more important than trade with the developed world. Developed nations are exporting less to each other and more proportionately to the emerging economies. Interestingly, one country to baulk this trend is the UK, which now exports less proportionately to countries in the emerging world than it did in the 1980s. As shown in Table 1 (see page 15), the big trading nations in the world continue to include the USA, Germany and Japan. These are now being joined by Brazil, India, Russia and, most notably, China.

In 2015, China overtook the USA as the largest economy in the world. The Chinese economy became worth US$17.6 trillion according to the IMF, whereas that of the USA was US$17.4 trillion. These figures are based on **purchasing power parity (PPP)**.

In October 2015, a new trade deal, the **Trans-Pacific Partnership (TPP)**, was agreed between 12 nations around the Pacific Ocean (USA, Canada, Japan, Malaysia, Chile, Peru, Mexico, Brunei, Singapore, Vietnam, Australia and New Zealand). The deal cut trade tariffs between these nations and aimed to set common standards in member countries. Under the deal, 98% of tariffs will be eliminated on a wide range of products including dairy products, beef, sugar, wine, rice, horticulture, seafood, manufactured products and energy. The countries of the TPP have over 800 million people and cover about 40% of the global economy. However, there is one major issue with the TPP deal — China is not a signatory, though it did say that it hoped the TPP pact 'could contribute to the Asia-Pacific region's trade, investment and economic growth'.

The IMF predicts that by 2020 the Chinese economy will be worth $26.98 trillion — 20% bigger than the USA at $22.3 trillion. However, longer-term financial forecasts from the IMF and others indicate that by 2100 India could overtake them both.

Exam tip
Use an atlas to locate all of the countries in these trading groups.

Purchasing power parity (PPP) Enables you to compare how much you can buy for your money in different countries. As money goes further in China than in the USA, the figure is adjusted upwards.

Differential access to markets

The trading agreements discussed above and the various other ways in which countries become involved in the dealings of other countries, whether by trade or aid, or a combination of both (as illustrated by China's dealings overseas), have impacted the economic and societal wellbeing of the people within those nations.

You should study examples of how differential access to markets impacts nations and people. One example could be at a national level, such as how different areas of Mexico are affected by their trading relationship with the USA. Another could be to examine how individuals can gain access to markets in order to raise their personal living standards. These are examined briefly below.

Mexico and NAFTA

There is a huge variation of incomes within Mexico as the country modernises. For example, economic productivity in Nuevo León, a heavily industrialised state close to the US border (capital Monterrey), is at level equivalent to that of South Korea. Here maquiladora are common. In the south of Mexico productivity is close to that of sub-Saharan Africa. The country's industrial clusters devoted to the manufacture of cars, planes, electric goods and electrical equipment — categories that between them account for two-thirds of Mexico's manufacturing exports, and thus for about 18% of GDP — are largely to be found in a band next to its northern border and in the central states to the south of it. These states account for about 70% of the country's 120 million population. These figures are largely due to the access to the North American market that the region possesses, resulting from NAFTA.

> **Exam tip**
>
> Study the nature and impact of the maquiladora in Mexico in more detail.

Microfinance schemes

Microfinance refers to a number of different financial products including:

- **microcredit:** the provision of small-scale loans to the poor, for example by credit unions
- **microsavings:** for example, voluntary local savings clubs provided by charities
- **microinsurance:** especially for people and businesses not traditionally served by commercial insurance, which can act as a safety net to prevent people from falling back into poverty after, for example, a harvest failure
- **payment management:** for managing remittance payments sent between individuals. One of the most well known mobile phone-based solutions is M-Pesa in east Africa.

Microcredit attempts to reduce poverty and has several key characteristics:

- It often provides small loans for the working capital requirements of the rural poor, especially women.
- There is minimal risk assessment of borrowers compared with commercial banks.
- Security is rarely demanded for the money.
- Based on the loan repayment history of the members, microfinance institutions can extend larger loans to the members repeatedly.

For many people, microfinance and microcredit are essential and produce many benefits for poor and low-income households. Microfinance can also help to unlock a community's entrepreneurial potential and allow them to access markets for their products. However, this type of money lending is not without its critics. There are sometimes problems in terms of maintaining manageable interest rates, gender inequalities (experts agree that women should be the primary focus), and being able to reach those in most need while still covering operational costs. There are also problems of people defaulting on their loans and the scheme losing its assets.

Transnational corporations

The traditional view of a transnational corporation (TNC) is a firm that has the power to coordinate and control operations in more than one country. Such organisations are hierarchical and usually have a recognisable home base incorporating the headquarters and research and development (R&D) arm in developed countries, with centres of production overseas. Over the last few decades TNCs have developed different forms and have moved into a wide range of activities:

- **Resource extraction:** particularly in the mining and oil and gas industries (for example, BP, Exxon, Royal Dutch Shell and Chevron).
- **Manufacturing:** in high-end products such as computers and electronics (Apple) and pharmaceuticals (GSK), large-volume consumer goods such as cars (Ford, Toyota) and tyres (Michelin), and mass-produced consumer goods with products such as cigarettes, drinks, foods and cosmetics (BAT, Fosters, Unilever, Kellogg's, L'Oréal).
- **Services:** banking and insurance (HSBC), supermarkets (Walmart), advertising (Saatchi), freight transport (Norbert Dentressangle), hotel chains (Radisson) and fast-food outlets (McDonald's, KFC).

As there are so many different types and well-known names of TNCs, several organisations seek to identify the largest, or the most successful, TNCs in the world. This task is far from easy as there are a number of criteria that could be used, such as profit, turnover, assets and brand success. Tables 3 to 5 illustrate three such surveys with the ten largest TNCs in each case, but the outcomes are not the same.

Table 3 is produced by *Forbes* (a US business magazine), where the top six TNCs are all in the financial sector, and the top four largest are Chinese banks. Table 4 shows the top ten TNCs with the financial sector taken out, this time produced by the website TopForeignstocks.com. It is noticeable here how oil companies and car companies dominate the table. Finally, Table 5 illustrates the marketing success of the brand of TNCs, according to *Fortune Global 500* (another US business magazine). This time, consumer companies dominate the list. Perhaps you will recognise more of the names in Table 5 than the other two, indicating the importance and success of their marketing strategies.

Exam tip

Here is a good example of where you can reflect on the impact of geographical phenomena on your life.

Knowledge check 7

Write about the success or otherwise of a microfinance scheme you have studied.

Transnational corporation (TNC) A company that operates in more than one country.

Table 3 The world's ten largest public TNCs (all categories) 2014

Rank	TNC (country of origin)
1	ICBC (China)
2	China Construction Bank (China)
3	Agricultural Bank of China (China)
4	Bank of China (China)
5	Berkshire Hathaway (USA)
6	JP Morgan Chase (USA)
7	ExxonMobil (USA)
8	PetroChina (China)
9	General Electric (USA)
10	Wells Fargo (USA)

Source: *Forbes*

Table 4 The world's ten largest non-financial TNCs 2014

Rank	TNC (country of origin)
1	General Electric (USA)
2	Royal Dutch Shell (UK)
3	Toyota (Japan)
4	ExxonMobil (USA)
5	Total SA (France)
6	BP (UK)
7	Vodafone (UK)
8	Volkswagen (Germany)
9	Chevron (USA)
10	Eni SpA (Italy)

Source: Topforeignstocks.com

Table 5 The world's ten largest TNCs by brand 2015

Rank	TNC (country of origin)
1	Apple (USA)
2	Samsung (Korea)
3	Google (USA)
4	Microsoft (USA)
5	Verizon (USA)
6	AT&T (USA)
7	Amazon (USA)
8	General Electric (USA)
9	China Mobile (China)
10	Walmart (USA)

Source: *Fortune Global 500*

Deeper analysis of some of these companies illustrates how the nature and role of TNCs has become much more complex. In particular, an important distinction has arisen between two different types of 'operation':

- **Genuine overseas branch plant operations**: production or retailing facilities resulting from FDI and owned by the parent company. An example would be Ford, a US car company with its headquarters in the USA, but having branch plants in countries such as the UK and Mexico.
- **Business arrangements known as global production networks (GPN)**: large corporations, ranging from Dell to Tesco, have established thousands of subcontracting partnerships while building their global businesses. The term 'transnational corporation' cannot cover this. A TNC that orchestrates a GPN can be described as a **hub company**.

As globalisation has accelerated, the size and density of GPNs have grown. GPNs span food, manufacturing, retailing, technology and financial services. Food giant Kraft and electronics firm IBM both have 30,000 suppliers providing the ingredients they need and helping to generate huge revenues. The world's largest firms have multiplied the size of their supply chains many times over through corporate mergers and acquisitions (for example, Kraft acquired the Cadbury's GPN in 2010, adding it to its own).

Global production network (GPN) A system whereby a TNC manages a series of suppliers and subcontracted partnerships while building its global business.

Social, economic and environmental impacts of TNCs

Impacts on the host country

The **advantages** of TNCs locating in a country are:

- **employment**
- **injection of capital into the local economy:** more disposable income will create a demand for more housing, transport and local services
- **multiplier effects:** investment by a TNC can trigger more employment through the process of cumulative causation bringing greater wealth into a region, e.g. component suppliers and distributors

Knowledge check 8

Explain how a hub company operates.

- **new working methods:** the transfer of technology will create a more skilled workforce. Also, new methods will be adopted, such as just-in-time (JIT) component supply and quality management systems.

The **disadvantages** are:
- **competition:** arrival of TNCs may have an adverse effect on local companies, which might not be as efficient
- **environmental concerns:** many developing countries have less stringent pollution laws than in the TNC's home country
- **labour exploitation:** many have alleged that some TNCs exploit cheap, flexible, non-unionised labour forces in developing countries. This has been strongly denied by many TNCs, which point to a basic standard of operation involving worker training facilities, and promotion opportunities for locals, with a minimum wage in force.
- **urbanisation:** establishing factories in major urban centres leads to their expansion as younger workers migrate from rural areas. This can also have serious consequences in those rural areas.
- **removal of capital:** to the TNC's home country
- **outside decision-making:** plans affecting plants in developing countries are made in the home country and usually for the benefit of the TNC and its profitability

Impacts on the country of origin
The **positive** impacts are:
- **high-salary employment:** even when TNCs move their operations overseas, the headquarters and R&D often stay in the home country
- **return of profits:** successful TNCs return their profits to the home country to be distributed among shareholders. Profits are also taxed, which increases government revenues.

Negative impacts are:
- **unemployment:** for both the TNC's employees and those in component suppliers
- **reverse multiplier effects:** as unemployment increases in a region, disposable income falls, leading to a downward spiral (vicious circle)

You are required to study a **specified TNC**, including its impact on those countries in which it operates.

World trade in a commodity or product
You are required to study the world trade in at least one food commodity or one manufactured product. Here is an example of the latter.

World trade in cars
During 2014, global car exports amounted to US$698.5 billion. This represented a 25.6% increase from 2010 to 2014. Table 6 summarises the main importers and exporters of cars in 2014. It is interesting to note that several countries feature in both

Just-in-time (JIT) A manufacturing system designed to minimise the costs of holding stocks of raw materials and components by carefully planned scheduling of deliveries.

Exam tip

It is important that you have an understanding of all four areas of impact, i.e. positive and negative impacts on the host country and positive and negative impacts on the country of origin.

lists, and that they are all developed countries or emerging economies. It is fair to conclude that the bulk of world trade in cars is between rich countries, where people have high disposable incomes.

At a larger scale, the EU is the second-largest importer and the largest exporter. It is worth noting too that the scandal that affected Volkswagen in the autumn of 2015 may impact on this European dominance. China and India are both significant producers of cars, but are not currently exporting significant amounts.

Table 6 Top ten car importers/exporters (2014)

Rank	Importers	% of world imports	Exporters	% of world exports
1	USA	22.4	Germany	22.9
2	China	8.5	Japan	12.7
3	Germany	6.6	USA	8.8
4	UK	6.6	Canada	6.4
5	France	4.4	South Korea	6.4
6	Canada	3.9	UK	6.1
7	Belgium	3.8	Mexico	4.6
8	Italy	3.3	Spain	4.6
9	Australia	2.3	Belgium	4.3
10	Spain	2.1	France	2.7

Source: WTO (2015)

Globalisation critique

As globalisation continues apace, and more and more parts of the world have the desire to raise the living standards of their people to a perceived level of expectation, it is apparent that economic development cannot rise smoothly alongside social, cultural and environmental development. Some have argued that globalisation helps to integrate the world, thereby maintaining peace and a level of stability. However, while it is in everyone's interest that people live under better conditions, it is also true that the richest among us, nations as well as individuals, want to maintain their differential, even if their desire to do so impacts negatively on others. Others believe that globalisation has created greater inequality, injustice, conflict and environmental degradation.

Globalisation and associated development can also depend on scale and location; it can be driven by decisions of world governance, national and regional governments, or it can be down to the decisions taken by groups and individuals in small communities. You should always consider this topic at different scales and from different points of view, including yours.

Exam tip

Examination questions are likely to ask you to analyse, discuss and evaluate. Be prepared to make assessments based on evidence.

Case studies

Only one case study is specified by this area of the specification — the study of a TNC — but it may be desirable to outline some areas within the material covered above where case studies would enhance your work.

1 The impacts of named TNCs and their activities in specified areas of the world to illustrate the social, economic and environmental outcomes of their activities. Try to ensure that you take a balanced approach, citing positive benefits as well as negative costs. It is always useful to consider how different people may view these impacts, as values and attitudes are important in this area of study.

2 A case study of a specified TNC. You should be able to identify its country of origin as well as the countries where it operates, or to which it subcontracts work (host countries). Consider its spatial organisation — areas of headquarters, R&D and production — and study the linkages within the company. You should also seek to evaluate its marketing strategies for the products it trades.

Summary

After studying this topic, you should be able to:
- understand the factors that have driven globalisation, and the various dimensions to it
- understand the form and nature of economic, political, social and environmental dependencies that have arisen in the world as a consequence of globalisation
- recognise and evaluate issues that have arisen, such as inequalities in flows of people, money, ideas, technology and in power relations
- know the main features and trends of global trade, including the major trading relationships and patterns that exist between nations and economic groupings
- analyse the degree to which differential access to markets is associated with levels of economic development, and how it impacts on economic and societal wellbeing
- evaluate the nature and role of TNCs and their impacts on the countries where they operate
- know the world trade in at least one commodity (food or manufactured)
- analyse and assess the geographical consequences of global systems, in particular world trade and access to markets, and how they impact your life and that of others
- debate the pros and cons of the impacts of globalisation by considering whether it has brought peace and stability, or injustice and inequality to the world

■ Global governance

General principles

Global governance refers to the emergence during the last 70 years or so of norms, rules, laws and institutions that have regulated and, to some extent, reproduced the trade-orientated global systems that were discussed in the previous section, as well as other global systems (such as those involving patterns of human development and population migration). These regulations have in turn had geographical consequences for the world's citizens and the places in which they live. Together global systems and global governance have shaped relationships between individuals, states and non-state organisations (for example, the United Nations (UN), transnational companies (TNCs) or non-governmental organisations (NGOs)) around the world.

Many of these systems and laws have been responsible for positive changes in the way in which global geopolitics operates. For example, UN-sponsored agreements on human rights and genocide coupled with international law were crucial in creating the post-1945 international system following the atrocities under Nazi Germany. Another agreement is where nation states, with exclusive sovereignty over their national territories, are treated as equal partners under the auspices of the UN Charter.

Global governance has dealt with issues such as those concerning trade (below), security, nuclear proliferation, legality, **human rights**, sovereignty and territorial integrity, the atmosphere, laws of the sea and the protection of animals. Some of these refer to what is known as the 'global commons' — the Earth's resources that are, in theory, shared by all.

> ### Exam tip
>
> The AQA specification concentrates on trade-related matters in the sections on global systems and global governance. You should also research global governance of one other area from the list above.

There have, however, been two significant issues associated with these attempts at global governance:

- How have agencies, including the UN in the post-1945 era, worked to promote growth and stability, and yet may have also created and exacerbated inequalities and injustices?
- How have the interactions between the local, regional, national and international, and global scales become fundamental to understanding the role of global governance?

The work of the UN will be examined later, but first let us seek to elaborate on the second issue in the context of trade.

All producers and consumers are linked with other people in other places and at different scales. Their interdependence and interactions are crucial for many of the world's systems. Although the power to act and to effect change is embedded in many different locations within the system(s), the most effective changes are often brought

Knowledge check 9

Summarise the main features of Article 1 of the UN Charter.

Human rights
Moral principles or norms that describe certain standards of human behaviour, and are protected as legal rights in international law.

about by different people or places working together in some form of partnership. Here is a list of some of the partners (sometimes referred to as 'actors') that can effect change at a global scale:

- **TNCs:** these can form or encourage cooperatives; they can source their materials and products ethically; they can enforce codes of conduct of their producers…or they can deliberately do none of these.
  - National governments can seek to regulate TNCs and these regulations can be replicated by other countries.
  - Supranational bodies such as the European Union (EU) and World Trade Organization (WTO) can regulate trade.
- **Workers:** these can form trade unions to defend their rights, both nationally and perhaps internationally; in extreme cases they can cite solidarity internationally.
- **Consumers:** consumers around the world can ask moral questions about the origin of food and other products, and they can reject exploitative goods.
- **Farmers:** can organise themselves into collectives, and have greater strength to negotiate as groups. An example of this is the Fairtrade movement (see below).
- **NGOs (such as Greenpeace, Oxfam):** can lobby, raise public awareness, fund projects and educate.

Finally, there have been some concerns expressed about the global governance of whatever is being governed, with several questions being raised:

- What is the purpose of the governing mechanisms? How and why were the particular agencies/partners brought together, and what are their interests and rationales?
- How well do the various agencies/partners work together?
- How well does global governance work, bearing in mind the different rates of economic, social and cultural development around the world?
- Just how democratic or accountable are these unelected, and largely appointed bodies and the people who run them? How does this square with increasing levels of inclusion and empowerment?

It should be noted that there is no guarantee of governance success, and there will always be concerns over the coordination, accountability and legitimacy of governance structures.

Examples of global governance

The development of trade agreements

The first major steps in the growth of today's level of international trade took place after the Second World War. The initial steps in opening up the global economy were made in the 1950s and 1960s as the desire to avoid the economic and political mistakes of the interwar period led to the gradual dismantling of trade barriers. Some of this was done within specific geographies — notably with the formation of the European Coal and Steel Community in 1951, the forerunner of the EU. Most, however, came about as a result of close cooperation between democratic powers keen to escape the conflicts of the first half of the twentieth century.

> **Exam tip**
>
> A consistent theme of human geography at A-level is how a concept impacts your life and that of others across the globe. You need to develop views and opinions, and the confidence to express them.

This resulted in:

- the Marshall Plan, which helped to deliver post-war reconstruction in a bid to avoid the mistakes contained within the Treaty of Versailles
- the delivery of a number of successful General Agreement on Tariffs and Trade (GATT) rounds designed to reduce trade barriers. GATT was replaced by the World Trade Organization (WTO) in 1995.
- the creation of the International Monetary Fund (IMF) and the World Bank
- the creation of the North Atlantic Treaty Organization (NATO), a response to fears of Soviet expansion in Europe (an example of global security governance being interdependent with trade governance)

Knowledge check 10

What is the purpose of NATO?

These collectively interconnected a series of systems and arrangements that were political, financial, economic and security-based in order to support trade. The consequence was a massive re-opening of world trade. However, only those countries that make up the core countries within the developed world, the OECD, really benefited.

Organisation for Economic Cooperation and Development (OECD) A group of economically developed countries that aims to promote policies which will improve the economic and social wellbeing of people around the world.

As the reforms took place between like-minded democracies, it seemed as though economic progress depended on democratic status. There is one major exception to this, and it remains so, to an extent: Singapore. Singapore's economy has gone from extreme poverty to considerable wealth in the space of 50 years even though it has no conventional democratic framework.

During the latter half of the twentieth century, more and more countries began to not only trade with, but also, through TNCs and government sources, invest in other countries (FDI).

In the initial stages, the rapid rise of FDI mostly affected wealthy (high-income) nations. Japan and Germany, with their large current account surpluses, mostly lent money to the USA. The USA ran a large current account deficit funded by ever-increasing surpluses in Germany and Japan. In return for this funding of the USA's deficit, the latter provided military and diplomatic protection for both countries in the midst of the Cold War. This is another example in which trade and security come together.

Foreign direct investment (FDI) Mostly by TNCs, but also increasingly by Sovereign Wealth Funds (money from governments).

At the end of the 1970s, Deng Xiaoping's China was beginning to 'open its doors' to the rest of the world and turning its back on the period under Chairman Mao. Similarly, India, which had previously protected inefficient domestic industries, began to re-connect with the West. Countries in Eastern Europe previously controlled by Soviet Russia rushed to join the EU. Countries in Latin America also wanted to join in the spirit of free trade — Mexico joined the North American Free Trade Agreement (NAFTA) and several Latin American nations formed Mercosur, another free trade union.

There can be no doubt that the world is much more closely interconnected by trade as a consequence of the opening up to business of much of the emerging world. An examination of the trading partners of both China and the USA (the world's largest economies) illustrates this well (see Tables 7 and 8).

Table 7 China's major trading partners (2013)

Rank	Exports (%)	Imports (%)
1	USA (17.2)	EU (11.7)
2	EU (16.3)	Japan (9.8)
3	Hong Kong (15.8)	South Korea (9.3)
4	Japan (7.4)	Hong Kong (7.9)
5	South Korea (4.3)	USA (7.4)

Source: WTO

Table 8 USA's major trading partners (2013)

Rank	Exports (%)	Imports (%)
1	Canada (18.8)	China (19.1)
2	EU (17.1)	EU (16.7)
3	Mexico (13.9)	Canada (14.0)
4	China (7.2)	Mexico (12.0)
5	Japan (4.5)	Japan (6.4)

Source: WTO

Exam tip

Summarise the main features of USA and Chinese trade as shown in Tables 7 and 8.

All of this is ultimately a reflection of the enhanced mobility of financial capital. Yet for all the economic progress made by the emerging world, the developed world, consisting of high-income countries, has strengthened its grip on the world economy. The world's leading financial centres are still New York, London and Tokyo. Emerging nations are, in investment terms, an adjunct to the making of money in the developed world. Indeed, as we have seen in London, super wealthy individuals from the emerging world, such as Russians, Saudis and Chinese, are more than willing to invest in real estate in the developed world. Even today there is little solid investment beyond manufacturing industry in the emerging world.

The United Nations

The United Nations (UN) is an international organisation designed to make the enforcement of international law, security, economic development, social progress and human rights easier for countries around the world. It includes 193 countries as its member states, and its main headquarters are located in New York, USA. The UN is the most representative intergovernmental organisation in the world today. It has made enormous positive contributions in maintaining international peace and stability, promoting cooperation among states and international development. The UN believes that only through international cooperation can mankind meet the challenges of these issues in the global and regional contexts. The UN plays a pivotal and positive role in this regard. However, some have pointed out that certain UN actions have actually exacerbated inequalities and injustices.

Exam tip

Research where in the world the UN currently has peacekeepers.

The UN operates through applying the principles of the Charter of the United Nations, and its main authority in maintaining international peace and security is through the Security Council. The UN states that to strengthen its role, it is essential to ensure for all member states the right to equal participation in international affairs, and that the rights and interests of the developing countries should be safeguarded. Although the UN does not maintain its own military, it does have peacekeeping forces, which its member states supply. On approval of the UN Security Council, these peacekeepers are often sent to regions where armed conflict has recently ended, in order to discourage combatants from resuming fighting.

Knowledge check 11

Through which agencies does the UN provide humanitarian assistance around the world?

In addition to maintaining peace, the UN aims to protect human rights and provide humanitarian assistance when needed. In 1948, the General Assembly adopted the Universal Declaration of Human Rights as a standard for its human rights operations. The UN currently provides technical assistance in elections, helps to improve judicial structures and draft constitutions, trains human rights officials, and provides food, drinking water, shelter and other humanitarian services to peoples displaced by famine, war and natural disaster.

In 2000, the UN established its **Millennium Development Goals (MDGs)**. Most of its member states and various international organisations agreed to achieve these goals relating to reducing poverty and child mortality, fighting diseases and epidemics, and developing a global partnership in terms of international development by 2015. Some member states have achieved a number of the agreement's goals while others have reached none. This is cited as one example where the UN may have exacerbated inequality around the world.

The **Sustainable Development Goals (SDGs)** were agreed in September 2015, with some targets similar to the MDGs, such as ending poverty and hunger, and others focused on combating the threat of global warming, and protecting oceans and forests from further degradation. To be successful, the SDGs will require a renewed UN system. A growing number of emerging nations will play an expanded role in this system, with probably a larger financial contribution, greater presence in governance, a stronger voice and a greater influence.

> **Millennium Development Goals (MDGs)** A series of targets set between 2000 and 2015 that aimed to act on the main causes of poverty around the world, including diet, education and disease.

> **Exam tip**
>
> You should examine the success or otherwise of one or two specific MDG targets.

Fairtrade

On a much smaller scale, **Fairtrade** is a social movement whose stated goal is to help producers in developing countries achieve better trading conditions and promote sustainability. Members of the movement advocate the payment of higher prices to exporters, as well as higher social and environmental standards. The movement focuses in particular on commodities, or products, that are typically exported from developing countries to developed countries, but also consumed in large domestic markets (such as Brazil and India), most notably coffee, cocoa, sugar, tea, bananas, cotton and chocolate. The movement seeks to promote greater equity in international trading partnerships through dialogue, transparency and respect. It promotes sustainable development by offering better trading conditions for, and securing the rights of, marginalised producers and workers in developing countries. It is an example of how smaller bodies — an NGO — can seek to exert governance on world trade.

> **Exam tip**
>
> You could research how Fairtrade seeks to influence world trade in products such as bananas, chocolate, coffee, beauty products and more.

> **Knowledge check 12**
>
> What is meant by the term 'ethical trade'?

Global trade talks

One common characteristic of global trade talks over the last 50 years under the auspices of the WTO has been the degree to which they have stumbled towards agreement. Over the years, the main stumbling blocks have been:

- The poor countries want a much greater reduction in subsidies for farmers in rich countries so that their own farm produce can compete in world markets.
- The rich countries want the poor countries to remove import levies on agricultural goods coming into poor countries.

Subsidy reductions would mean some hardships for producers such as US cotton farmers and EU dairy and sugar farmers, as they would be threatened by cheaper imports from the developing world. Poor countries in turn worry that if they remove their trade levies their own farmers would never be able to compete with cheaper imported agricultural products from developed countries. In addition, poorer countries get a large proportion of their tax revenues from taxing imports.

Some countries are very poor and need help to develop their trade. This includes protection of their fledgling processing industries from cheaper imports of processed goods, and richer countries sharing their technical expertise and knowledge to bring them up to twenty-first-century trading standards. These countries needed economic support to attain the MDGs, and will need it to attain the SDGs in the future.

The 'global commons'

The term 'global commons' was first used in the *World Conservation Strategy*, a report on conservation published in 1991 by the International Union for Conservation of Nature and Natural Resources (IUCN) in collaboration with the United Nations Educational, Scientific and Cultural Organization (UNESCO), the United Nations Environment Programme (UNEP) and the World Wildlife Fund (WWF). It stated:

> A commons is a tract of land or water owned or used jointly by the members of a community. The global commons include those parts of the Earth's surface beyond national jurisdictions — notably the open ocean and the living resources found there, or held in common, notably the atmosphere. The only landmass that may be regarded as part of the global commons is Antarctica.

Global commons
The Earth's shared resources, such as the deep oceans, the atmosphere, outer space and Antarctica.

The report stated that all people on the planet have a right to the benefits of the global commons. It also stated that, bearing in mind the right of all people to sustainable development, the global commons require protection. The protection of one of the major global commons — the atmosphere — is explained in the *Component 1: Physical geography* Student Guide. You may want to revisit those sections examining the human interventions in the carbon cycle that seek to mitigate climate change.

More recently, the internet and the resultant notion of cyberspace have been linked to the concept of the global commons. It will be interesting to see if global governance is, or can be, enforced in this aspect of human living.

Exam tip

Consider ways in which the internet is being, or can be, managed in the world today, but also think about how difficult this is becoming for authorities.

Management of the global commons

The key challenge of the concept of the global commons is the design of governance structures and management systems capable of addressing the complexity of multiple public and private interests. Management of the global commons requires a range of legal entities, usually international and supranational, public and private, structured to match the diversity of interests and the types of resource to be managed. They should be stringent but with adequate incentives to ensure compliance. The purpose of such global management systems is to avoid a situation whereby the resources held in common become overexploited.

In general, many of the global commons (the atmosphere, Antarctica) are non-renewable on human time scales. Thus, resource degradation is more likely to be the result of unintended consequences that are unforeseen, not immediately observable or not easily understood. For example, the carbon dioxide and methane emissions that drive climate change will continue to do so for at least a millennium after they enter the atmosphere, while species extinctions last forever.

Several environmental protocols have been established as a form of international law. These have tended to be intergovernmental documents intended as legally binding with a primary stated purpose of preventing or managing human impact on natural resources. International environment protocols have come to feature with the governance of trans-boundary environmental problems, such as acid rain in the late 1950s and 1960s.

However, environmental protocols are not a panacea for global commons issues. Often they are slow to produce the desired effects, and lack monitoring and enforcement. They also take an incremental approach to solutions where sustainable development principles suggest that environmental concerns should be mainstream political issues.

Antarctica as a global commons

The geography of Antarctica and the Southern Ocean

Antarctica is the Earth's most southern continent, containing the geographic South Pole. It is almost entirely south of the Antarctic Circle and is surrounded by the Southern Ocean. (Note: the AQA specification includes the Southern Ocean as far north as the Antarctic Convergence). Its size is estimated to be 14 million km^2, making it the fifth-largest continent. It is twice the size of Australia. A total of 98% of the land area is covered by ice, which averages almost 2 km in thickness, and this ice extends to all but the most northern reaches of the Antarctic Peninsula.

Antarctica is the coldest, driest and windiest of all of Earth's continents, and has the highest average elevation. Climatically, it is a desert, with an annual precipitation of only 200 mm along the coast and lower totals inland. Around the coasts temperatures are generally close to freezing in the summer months (December–February), or even slightly positive in the northern part of the Antarctic Peninsula. During winter, monthly mean temperatures at coastal stations are between −10°C and −30°C but temperatures may briefly rise towards freezing when winter storms bring warm air towards the Antarctic coast.

Conditions on the high interior plateau are much colder as a result of its higher elevation, higher latitude and greater distance from the ocean. Here, summer temperatures struggle to get above −20°C and monthly means fall below −60°C in winter.

The distribution of precipitation over Antarctica is varied, with several metres of snow falling each year near the coast, but the interior only getting an annual snowfall of a few centimetres, thus officially making much of the continent a desert. After the snow has fallen the wind redistributes it, particularly in the coastal areas where downslope katabatic winds blow. The continent generally experiences moderate winds, with mean wind speeds of around 6 ms^{-1}, but in gales, which can occur on over 40 days a year, mean speeds can exceed 30 ms^{-1} with gusts of over 40 ms^{-1}.

Knowledge check 13

What is the Antarctic Convergence?

Exam tip

Research the climate data for one or more sites on Antarctica, such as Vostok, one of the coldest places on Earth.

The strong katabatic winds, caused by the flow of cold air off the central plateau, make some coastal sites around Antarctica the windiest places in the world.

There are no permanent human residents, but between 1000 and 5000 scientists live there at any one time at research stations scattered across the continent. There is a variety of flora and fauna present, consisting of algae, bacteria, fungi, and some plants and animals ranging in size from mites and nematodes to penguins and seals. Where vegetation does occur it can be classed as tundra.

Antarctica is governed by parties to the Antarctic Treaty System (ATS), each of which has consulting status. Twelve countries signed the Antarctic Treaty in 1959, and since then a further 38 have signed. The treaty prohibits military activities, mineral mining, nuclear explosions and nuclear waste disposal. It supports scientific research, and protects the continent's ecology. The intention of the treaty is to protect the continent's vulnerability to the threats from both economic pressures and environmental change.

Threats to Antarctica

Climate change

The Intergovernmental Panel on Climate Change (IPCC) stated the following in 2013 regarding Antarctic regions:

> The average rate of ice loss from the Antarctic ice sheet has likely increased from 30 Gt yr^{-1} over the period 1992–2001 to 147 Gt yr^{-1} over the period 2002–2011. There is very high confidence that these losses are mainly from the northern Antarctic Peninsula and the Amundsen Sea sector of West Antarctica.

> It is very likely that the annual mean Antarctic sea ice extent increased at a rate in the range of 1.2–1.8% per decade (range of 0.13–0.20 million km^2 per decade) between 1979 and 2012.

Exam tip

Keep up to date with what the IPCC states about climate change in Antarctica.

The impact of climate change will vary across the continent (Figure 1):

(a) The East Antarctic Ice Sheet (EAIS) is thought to be very stable due to its extremely cold temperatures. If the temperature increased by a few degrees it is still far too cold for surface melting, and so the ice sheet would not shrink. Only if the temperature went up by huge amounts (tens of degrees) would it be possible for major melting to begin. Most scientists working on the Antarctic ice sheets think that the EAIS will not collapse or cause a significant sea-level rise for many centuries to come.

(b) The West Antarctic Ice Sheet (WAIS) is the opposite — it is unstable. The fact that much of the ice sits below sea level means that it is sensitive to small rises in sea level, which can cause it to thin. Moreover, the WAIS is drained by several ice streams — fast-moving 'rivers' of ice very different from the slow-moving ice of the rest of the Antarctic ice sheets on the EAIS. Because they move so fast, and drain so much of the ice in the WAIS, the ice streams have the potential to rapidly increase the amount of ice being lost from the ice sheet to the ocean.

(c) The Antarctic Peninsula (AP) is one of the most rapidly warming places in the world. Air temperatures here have increased by 3°C over the last 50 years. This warming has been associated with the strengthening of the winds that encircle Antarctica, which in turn drives changes in oceanic circulation and increased upwelling of circumpolar deep water within the Southern Ocean. Across the AP, some 87% of glaciers are receding. The most pronounced impact has been the collapse of some AP ice shelves. Warmth has caused extra melting on the surface of the ice shelves, and eventually this leads to break-up. Recent research using aerial photographs and satellite imagery has shown that nearly 90% of the glaciers in the AP have retreated since they were first measured.

> **Exam tip**
>
> Use an atlas to locate and assess the relative sizes of the EAIS, WAIS and AP.

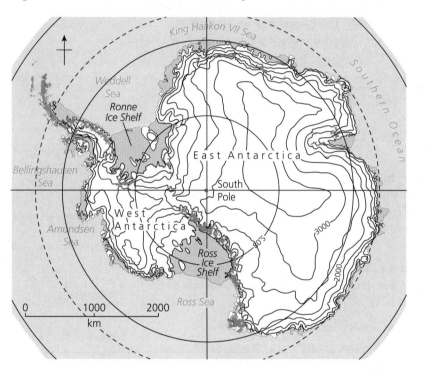

Figure 1 Antarctica

Fishing and whaling

Whaling for meat oil and whalebone resulted in whaling stations for meat processing being set up in the late nineteenth century on the islands of South Georgia and South Shetland in the Southern Ocean. As whales, especially the blue whale, began to die out, many countries stopped the trade.

Fishing became the main economic use of the seas during the 1960s and 1970s, during which large Russian and Japanese fishing fleets fished rock cod and krill stocks using industrial-scale trawlers. However, by the late 1970s these fisheries had collapsed. Subsequently, through the 1980s and to the present day the dominant exploited biomass is krill.

All these fisheries are now regulated through the Convention for the Conservation of Antarctic Marine Living Resources (CCAMLR), which came into existence in 1982. A central objective of Antarctic marine research is to provide scientific support for the work of CCAMLR. It is suggested that the place of krill in the ecology of the area is crucial — if the krill disappear, the entire food chain will collapse.

Knowledge check 14

What are krill and why are they important for the food chain?

The search for mineral resources

The initial Antarctic Treaty did not address the regulation of mineral resource activities. There are many Antarctic resources as yet undeveloped, including oil, coal and many metals. The UK and New Zealand first raised the issue of control of possible future mining within the ATS in 1970, as mineral companies had approached the two countries regarding possible commercial geophysical exploration in the Southern Ocean. The regulation of mineral activities has become a very controversial issue.

The issue was so difficult and complex that it took until 1988 for the Treaty nations to reach a consensus and adopt the Convention on the Regulation of Antarctic Mineral Resource Activities (CRAMRA). CRAMRA sought to regulate mineral prospecting, exploration and development activities. Mining would only be permitted if all parties agreed that there was no risk to the environment.

However, due to intense pressure from environmental groups, Australia and France decided not to sign CRAMRA. As the CRAMRA required ratification by all the Treaty nations, this meant that the agreement failed to come into force. By 1990, New Zealand, Italy and Belgium had joined these nations and together they proposed a comprehensive environmental protection convention for Antarctica. Others, including the UK, Japan and the USA, argued against a permanent ban on mining. A new Protocol on Environmental Protection to the Antarctic Treaty was signed in 1991. The Environmental Protocol now bans all mineral resource activities in Antarctica (other than for scientific research).

Tourism and scientific research

The development of small-scale tourism began in Antarctica in the 1950s, with commercial tour operators providing passenger ships. The first specially designed, ice-strengthened cruise ship, the *Lindblad Explorer*, visited in 1969. Since then the industry has grown considerably, with numbers of tourists increasing from under 9,000 in 1992/93 to over 50,000 in 2012/13. Tourists go to see the wildlife and, as this activity is relatively small-scale, it could be argued to be sustainable. However, the summer is the breeding season for most Antarctic wildlife and disturbance could upset the balance. There is also pressure on the landing sites that receive most tourists, especially the old whaling stations and historic sites such as McMurdo Sound, where the original huts from Scott's expedition in 1912 are located.

All tour operators providing visits to Antarctica are members of the International Association of Antarctica Tour Operators (IAATO), which seeks to ensure that tourism in Antarctica is conducted in an environmentally friendly way. The British Antarctic Survey (BAS) also welcomes a small number of visits to its stations during the austral summer, and groups are given a guided tour of the facilities, where they have the opportunity to learn about the scientific research the BAS undertakes.

Exam tip

Research the British Antarctic Survey (BAS), and, in particular, find out where it has bases on Antarctica.

Governance of Antarctica

Some aspects of the governance of Antarctica have been mentioned previously, including the ATS and Protocol on Environmental Protection to the Antarctic Treaty. Further detail will be provided here, but you should also assess the geographical consequences of these forms of governance for the citizens who work on Antarctica, and for the places that form the continent.

As elsewhere in human geography, you should also consider how these aspects of global governance impact your life and the lives of other people across the globe.

1 The Antarctic Treaty System (ATS) 1959

The ATS is a whole complex of arrangements to ensure:

> ...in the interests of all mankind that Antarctica shall continue forever to be used exclusively for peaceful purposes and shall not become the scene or object of international discord.

It prohibits 'any measures of a military nature', but does 'not prevent the use of military personnel or equipment for scientific research or for any other peaceful purpose'.

In 2004, the permanent secretariat to the ATS commenced its work in Buenos Aires, Argentina. The ATS covers the area south of 60°S latitude. Its objectives are simple yet unique in international relations. They are:

- to demilitarise Antarctica, to establish it as a zone free of nuclear tests and the disposal of radioactive waste, and to ensure that it is used for peaceful purposes only
- to promote international scientific cooperation in Antarctica
- to set aside disputes over territorial sovereignty.

2 The Protocol on Environmental Protection (Madrid Protocol) 1991

Another method used to implement Antarctic policy has been to conclude an international treaty connected to the original Antarctic Treaty. This occurred after France and Australia abandoned the CRAMRA as a solution to the mining issue and the need arose to find a new convention. The background to the Protocol is given above, and its main purpose is its Article 4, namely to put in law the three ATS objectives mentioned above.

3 The United Nations (UNEP)

The United Nations Environment Programme's (UNEP) direct involvement in Antarctic matters includes the preparation of a regular report for the UN Secretary-General on Antarctica. In order to keep the international community informed on the activities of the Antarctic Treaty parties, the UN was requested to serve as a neutral channel in order to provide information on Antarctic activities. To this end, the UN Secretary-General submits to the UN General Assembly a report on the 'Question of Antarctica' on a periodical basis, usually every three years. UNEP prepares the report.

Knowledge check 15

What is the role of the International Whaling Commission?

Exam tip

Research the work of NGOs such as the Scientific Committee on Antarctic Research (SCAR), the Antarctic and Southern Ocean Coalition (ASOC) and the Antarctic Oceans Alliance.

4 The role of non-governmental organisations

Several non-governmental organisations (NGOs) have an active interest in the protection of the Antarctic and its surrounding ocean and islands. Due to the constraints of the ATS, they can undertake very little in terms of direct impact. Their major involvement, therefore, has been to ensure that the various protocols and regulatory bodies mentioned above are enforced, and that they are active in monitoring threats and enhancing protection.

Summary

After studying this topic, you should be able to:
- understand the emergence and developing role of various forms of global governance
- evaluate issues such as trade and security associated with attempts at global governance
- know and appreciate the concept of the 'global commons, and illustrate it with particular reference to Antarctica
- know the contemporary geography of Antarctica and appreciate its vulnerability to a variety of environmental and economic threats
- analyse the threats facing Antarctica, such as climate change and tourism
- evaluate the various forms of global governance of Antarctica, either at a global scale or through NGOs
- reflect on the geographical consequences of global governance and how they impact your life and the lives of others

■ Changing places

This element of the new A-level course may strike many students and teachers alike as being very different from previous geographical experiences. It introduces a different way of looking at the places in which we and others live. Essentially, there are two sections to the work to be undertaken: a theoretical investigation of place, and application of that theory to real places. You are required to examine in detail two such places: one, a local place in which you live or may have based yourself on a field study; the other, a contrasting place. This second place could either be in the same or a different country from the first place, but it must show a significant contrast in terms of economic development and/or population density and/or cultural background and/or systems of political and economic organisation.

Some suggest that the better way to tackle this work is to undertake the second part — the investigation into real places — first. This book will examine the theory first, and then the investigations, thus following the sequence provided by the AQA specification.

The nature and importance of places

The concept and importance of place

There are many ways to consider the concept of 'place'. 'Place' is where someone was brought up, lives and may eventually die, and contains features that are unique to each individual. A place is more than just a **location**. Try this technique: ask each of your friends, family and acquaintances what their 'place' means to them. We all see places differently.

> **Location** A point in space with specific links to other points in space.

The definition of place, like any concept, is contested. At its heart, though, lies the notion of a meaningful segment of geographical space. We tend to think of places as settlements, for example, Doncaster, Dudley or Dartford. We also consider areas of cities or neighbourhoods — Harrow (London) or Longsight (Manchester) — to be places. Closer in, well-known public spaces are referred to as places, such as Covent Garden or Land's End. We may refer to a restaurant or café as a 'favourite place'. We also use expressions such as 'knowing one's place' or being 'put in our place' to suggest a more abstract and less locatable interaction of the social and the geographical. We have 'places' set at the dinner table and usually one of them is ours. We may have a favourite chair as our 'place'. We often have our favourite 'places' at school.

> **Exam tip**
>
> Create in your notes a series of 'places' that are important, or well known, at a variety of scales. They will be useful in supporting your arguments.

The latter notions begin to connect with the importance of place in our lives and experiences. At this point can 'place' take on a larger scale? Is 'place' important to us regionally — some people are proud Cornishmen, or Lancastrians — or nationally — the Welsh and the Scots? What of our 'place' in Europe? How many of us regard ourselves as European rather than British? Beyond the scale of the nation, environmental activist groups work to make us think of the Earth as a place — as a home for humanity — rather than a space to be exploited. Place, then, is not scale-specific. It can be as small as a setting at a table and as large as the Earth. The common assumption that place is a settlement is but one definition of place, and not the most interesting.

So, we must also consider the subjective aspects of a place, and not just the objective. This leads us to refer to a 'sense of place'. This refers to the feelings evoked by a place for both the **insiders** (people who live there) and **outsiders** (people who visit the area). Do we, for example, all have the same feelings when we visit an art gallery? Some feelings will be shared — the wonder of the paintings on display; some will be individual — as to how each painting affects us. We could perhaps reapply the technique used in the first paragraph of this section.

Places, then, are particular combinations of material things that occupy a particular segment of space and have sets of meanings attached to them. To paraphrase a well-known saying: 'A place for everyone and everyone in her/his place.'

Insider and outsider perspectives on place

Geographers studying place refer to **insider** and **outsider** perspectives. Insiders are said to develop a sense of place through their everyday experiences in familiar settings — daily rhythms (e.g. the school run) and shared experiences (e.g. socialising at the village pub) are critical and they underpin the subjectivity that is the basis for the community's sense of place. For outsiders, the sense of place is more vague and abstract. The outsider's view is often about discovery, a personal view of entering a location or landscape and learning about that place. The insider's view is usually about experience, a narrative of close involvement with the landscape and locale, expressing what time and repetition teach the person about that place. The insider is an inhabitant, a dweller; the outsider is a traveller, an observer from beyond the place.

The insider's advantage is that understanding accumulates, and is acquired by just living there rather than direct investigation. The feeling of 'place' emerges from a deeper, broader sense of familiarity. The outsider's advantage is to be able to see things afresh, to ask questions that the inhabitants don't think to ask because the answers are so familiar. They draw on experiences of other places to understand the one under observation. One perspective is intimate; the other is neutral. These images are important as they create generalisations and influence decisions regarding things such as investment, and whether to reside there, or to holiday there.

Categories of place

Various cultural geographers have tried to categorise places. Some categories include '**far places**', '**near places**', '**experienced places**' and '**media places**'. Perhaps these are best illustrated by the following.

Consider a village near Banbury in rural 'middle' England where people of different social groups live. At one extreme of the community there are highly educated academics, scientists and business people, mainly men, whose work is based in the nearby city of Oxford, although they all have computers with fast wifi at home. These people are in constant contact with, and physically travelling between, colleagues and customers all around the world. The spaces that they move in, both physically and virtually, are thoroughly global (**far places**). At the other extreme of the scale are people who have never been to London and have only rarely made it as far as Oxford, in order to go to the shops or maybe to the hospital. Members of this group are known as the 'locals', and most of them work on farms or in village shops and services (**near places**).

A sense of place The subjective feelings associated with living in a place.

Knowledge check 16

The term 'locale' is sometimes used in place geography. What does it mean?

Exam tip

You may be asked to define and/or elaborate on each of these terms to do with 'place'. Compile a table that summarises their main elements.

Other people in these villages work more or less locally, but are employed as cleaners or caterers by multinational firms, for which this is just one group of workers among many scattered across the globe. Finally, there are women (mostly) who are the partners of the men, several of whom are occupied in a daily round of nurseries and child-minders, often being the heart and soul of local meetings and charities (**near places**). They tend to drive into Oxford to do their shopping, maintain contacts with extended family outside the local area and like to go on holiday to somewhere 'exotic' (**far places**).

This account of the different social groups in this hypothetical village shows how place is far more permeable for some (the wealthy incomers and out-goers) than it is for others. In addition, within that social grouping there are gender differences in the shaping of activities within the place. However, even the more rooted, less-travelled, lower income people here are increasingly touched by wider events. Farm workers, for example, are subject to agricultural policy decisions made in London or Brussels, and the cleaners and caterers who work for multinational firms in the area might well feel the force of global economics if those companies were to cut back on jobs (all **experienced places**).

Add to these the assertion that in today's electronic society people have no 'sense of place'; rather, they occupy **media places**. Electronic media are undermining the traditional relationship between a physical setting and a social setting. The world's media bring to our location events that are taking place in another location, and hence in some ways we are transported to that location even though we actually remain in our own location. At a much smaller scale is the situation in which two people are having a telephone or a Skype conversation in two different locations. Indeed, the telephone (or computer) brings them closer together than with other people in their respective locations.

Factors contributing to the character of places

Endogenous factors

These are the starting points, or underpinning elements, of a place study based on accessible knowledge of the area, such as its location, topography and other aspects of the physical site, as well as the built environment (land use) and infrastructure. These factors also include social and economic characteristics, which determine the character of, and present a sense of identity, or meaning to, the place. They can involve processes both in the past as well as the present.

Exogenous factors

All places are affected by, and have relationships with, other places, or external factors. **Exogenous factors** are often associated with globalisation, and have affected a place because of their tendency to accelerate cultural homogenisation. For example, there may have been significant moves into the place of resources, capital, investment and ideas, and of course people from other places, some of which are international. These flows often affect the demographic, socioeconomic and cultural characteristics of the receiving place.

> **Knowledge check 17**
>
> All of these categories of place owe their origin to the ideas of Yi-Fu Tuan. He developed the phrase 'field of care'. What is the 'field of care'?

Endogenous factors
Factors that are caused or originate from within, i.e. internally.

Exogenous factors
Factors that are caused or have an origin from without, i.e. externally.

Your studies of 'place'

At the heart of this topic are the two detailed case studies of local places (one in which you live or study and one further contrasting place) that you must complete. When reading the following two sections (Relationships and connections, and Meaning and representation), ensure that you appreciate how the factors mentioned therein affect continuity and change in your chosen places. Also, reflect on how your life and that of others has been and is affected by such continuity and change in your places.

Relationships and connections

Places in a dynamic world

Tourist places are an obvious example of where flows of people and investment may have shaped the character of a place in a dynamic world. They illustrate how the demographic, socioeconomic and cultural characteristics of places are shaped by the shifting flows of people, resources, money, investment and ideas.

Tourism produces a distinctive set of interconnections between places because of its different relationships between producers and consumers. Whereas most consumers of goods rarely see or even know the producers of those goods (do you know who produces the wheat for your bread, for instance?), in tourist places, tourist consumers and the producers of tourist experiences often meet face to face.

In addition, the product that is sold at tourist sites is very often intangible. The tourist product is an experience that cannot physically be taken home. Tourism involves the visual consumption of a place, through a 'tourist gaze' that is unique to the individual tourist. Incomes are generated through the flow of images, information and experiences. In turn, the experiential nature of production and consumption actually shapes the material and sociocultural characteristics of the tourist place itself. Resources, money and investment all flow into the place, which further determine the nature of its characteristics, beyond the original endogenous factors that created it in the first place.

As an extreme example, perhaps, it could be argued that Ibiza and Verona are both attractive to the tourist interested in music. But that is perhaps the only comparison between the two places.

Forces of change

We must also consider the external forces, and **agents of change**, creating the changes in the place being studied. At a general level these are the individuals, community groups, institutions, multinational corporate bodies and various levels of government that have shaped the place over time. As already stated, the media and other forms of communication can also shape the way in which the place is perceived both from within and beyond the place, nationally as well as globally.

Returning to the tourist place scenario, tourism has been shaped by agents ranging from large travel companies, who decide which countries and locations to 'open up'

Exam tip

Consider the place in which you live. What are the endogenous and exogenous factors that have contributed to its growth? You can use these to illustrate exam answers.

Knowledge check 18

To what extent does globalisation impact 'place'?

Agents of change
Individuals, groups, multinational corporations, institutions (national or international), media and governments that have driven change either intentionally or unintentionally.

for mass tourism, to individual waiters and guides, who mould the experience of visiting consumers. Agents are also involved in the production of the infrastructure of the area, in transport, accommodation and the management of the environments being visited. Tourism also involves imaginative marketing and advertising — the people who endow Paris with the image of being 'romantic', Goa with being 'relaxing' and Ibiza with being 'cool' and yet 'exciting'. Travel advertisements, guidebooks, photographs and films all construct space in ways that structure its subsequent development as a tourist place. It can also be suggested that as tourism consumption changes, with more demand for niche-marketed destinations as well as mass destinations, agents will play a greater role. Consider, for example, the increase in adventure travel practices (e.g. bungee jumping and white water rafting) in places such as New Zealand.

Finally, we must not forget the role national governments play. They designate and protect particular areas in which the visual and active consumption of nature is undertaken. An interesting example is the role the French government played in regulating the development of Disneyland Paris. They influenced its built landscape, its management of waste and also the rights of its workers. They even overruled Disney in allowing its workers to wear lipstick, contrary to the rules in the USA.

Places in context

Places should also be studied in their context, for example, how past and present connections have shaped them and embedded them in regional, national, international and global contexts. The impact of this will vary from place to place; all places have a history that has shaped their development, but that history may be more significant for some places than others. Another key point here is to appreciate the complexity of the human environment. As geographers, we are interested in more than just the economic significance of places. They are places of political, cultural and social significance, too. Politics, religion, culture, history and so on all influence the make-up of a place. In fact, geographers often describe places as being made up of a series of layers, or as a **palimpsest** (something that has changed over time and shows evidence of that change), which can be unravelled in order to develop a greater appreciation of the place. For example, Istanbul is best understood when we think about the layers of history that influence the cityscape, from its links with the Greeks and the Ottoman Empire to its contemporary relationships with Europe and Asia.

At a smaller scale, the state, and even local government, can use place and space to assert power and ideology. Many capital cities and smaller cities and towns have public places, such as large open streets, parks and squares, which have played a role in asserting power and maintaining order. At varying times, these public places have also had a non-political role, which also defines the place.

Palimpsest Something that has been reused or altered but still bears visible traces of its earlier form.

Knowledge check 19

Having completed this part of the topic, now distinguish between 'location' and 'a sense of place'.

Exam tip

Consider the place in which you live. What are the public places created in your area, and what was/is their purpose? You can use these to illustrate exam answers.

Meaning and representation

Acquiring, developing and communicating a sense of place

This section examines how people perceive, engage with and form attachments to places. It also looks at how places present themselves to others and how they are represented to the rest of the world. Key concepts within this area of study are identity, belonging, ownership and wellbeing in relation to place. Perspectives and experiences of place are also key features of this area of study.

Identity and **belonging** are often judged by the external and internal characteristics of the person, such as class, gender, race, sexuality, marital status, religion and physical (dis)ability. Some writers believe that as biology directly determines many of these factors, then they are relatively fixed and stable. For example, some suggest that those such as single mothers or black youths have a particular common set of identities. On the other hand, others have stated that such views are inherently sexist or racist and can produce stereotyping. These writers argue that differences between us are shaped through the interweaving of wider socioeconomic processes. We should not assume that all single mothers share any common characteristic other than their gender and marital status, and we should be wary of labelling black youths, as such labels are often applied indiscriminately to demonise whole groups of people.

Some aspects of identity are political and emotional, and bring about feelings of being part of a group, belonging or otherwise. Inclusion or exclusion can then lead to feelings of discrimination, prejudice or injustice. Issues such as racism, sexism, homophobia and elitism are associated with identity and belonging. These are often both reflected and reinforced in space and place. Think, for example, of the Canal Street 'gay district' of Manchester, or the 'posh' district of Mayfair in London.

Identity, therefore, is formed in relation to others. We become aware of who we are through a sense of shared identity with others (such as speaking the same language, or having the same political views), and by a process of setting ourselves apart from those we consider different from ourselves. Identity can also have a degree of fluidity, or flux. With time our identities may change as, for example, our social class changes.

Ownership refers to the feeling of being in possession of a set of values, or a particular identity and, if desirable, it then adds to our sense of wellbeing and worth. Once again this takes us into the role of processes of inclusion and exclusion. The connection between place and particular meanings and identities leads to the notion of places in which it is possible to be either 'in place' or 'out of place' — an insider or an outsider. Things, practices and people labelled as out of place are said to have transgressed often-invisible boundaries that define what is appropriate and what is inappropriate. Young people gather on street corners or skateboard on street furniture; the homeless find ways to live in inhospitable places; street-artists (such as the well-known Banksy) redecorate urban walls to establish new meanings and identities in those communities. On a much larger scale the mass migrations of refugees that

Representation of place The cultural practices by which human societies interpret and portray the world around them and present themselves to others.

Identity An assemblage of personal characteristics such as gender, sexuality, race and religion.

Belonging A sense of being part of a collective identity.

Ownership The feeling of being in possession of a set of values, or a particular identity.

Wellbeing The positive outcome of a shared identity and a sense of belonging.

Knowledge check 20

Identify some of the varying identities of people involved in the European migration crisis of 2015/16.

Exam tip

You may be asked to define and/or elaborate on the terms 'identity' and 'representation'. Compile a table that summarises their main elements.

took place across Europe in the summer of 2015 challenged the whole concept of boundaries and national place. In general, whatever kinds of places are constructed, they are never truly finished and always open to question and transformation.

How places may be represented

Geographers have often pointed to the importance of the creative imagination to the ways in which we respond to places. They have made claims of the power of novels, poems, songs, the visual arts and other diverse media (television, film, photography, song) to 'bring alive' different places. You may have read a novel set in a place that has also been the subject of a case study in a textbook. In conventional terms the novel is fictional while the case study is factual, so it is worth reflecting on the different kinds of knowledge and understanding of that place that you have taken from each of them. All forms of literature and media can give contrasting images to that presented more formally or statistically, such as through cartography or census data.

You are encouraged to be open to the interpretation of texts, visual imagery, music and other cultural phenomena. They can indicate the ways in which local cultures shape their ideas about the relationships between humans and the natural world in that place; they provide another **representation** of place. Indeed, researchers in these disciplines are also exploring the significance of geography in their work. It is a two-way process.

Perhaps one of the strongest illustrations of the power of the written word when combined with imagery is in the world of advertising, such as the material tourist boards and agencies produce. Advertising depends on a combination of visual and written rhetoric, and particularly on the real and/or imaginary settings in which places are described and portrayed. This concept is not new. In the early twentieth century, railway companies produced many posters to advertise faraway places, accessible by train.

Exam tip

Consider how twenty-first-century advertisers entice consumers to tourist locations.

An advertisement will try to transport you somewhere else in space and time, sometimes to a past and/or distant world, where the natural value of the place is somewhat fanciful, yet touchable. However, do the representations of place through such media match the direct experience of people who live there?

Art and literature are not the only mediums where this works. Radio, television and other digital communication media can also adopt this approach to have an impact on 'place'. They make it possible for audiences in multiple, dispersed local settings to be in two places at once. Of course, it is only ever possible for any individual to be in one place at a time physically, but broadcasting permits a witnessing of remote happenings that can bring certain events or places experientially 'close' or 'within range', thereby removing the 'farness'. The impact of television on the tourist prospects of several locations can be highlighted here; for example, think of the effect of programmes such as *Inspector Morse*, *Broadchurch* and *Doc Martin* on their respective settings of Oxford, Dorset and Cornwall.

Exam tip

All of these locations are UK based. Think of several overseas locations in which various forms of media have highlighted their worth (or otherwise).

Management and manipulation of the perception of place

Some organisations attempt to manage, or even manipulate, the perception of place for their own ends. This is not always as sinister as it may seem, but instead is aimed at managing how others see work being undertaken in a community in order to improve the place, or to raise awareness of what is being done. External agencies, such as community groups dealing with local health issues, corporate bodies who are keen to raise awareness of new developments taking place, and local and national governments, all try to manipulate place perception to varying degrees in order to achieve further policy ends. Perhaps the best example of all three of these types of body working together is in a partnership of non-governmental and governmental organisations aimed at developing or regenerating an area. Examples include Cardiff Bay (Europe's largest waterfront development, in the Welsh capital), Salford Quays (another waterfront development, in Great Manchester) and the Ocean Gateway Project (sometimes referred to as the Atlantic Gateway, which will involve extensive redevelopment of the Port of Liverpool and the Manchester Ship Canal).

The attraction of partnerships results from their apparent potential to bring together interested local organisations, including businesses, and agents of government in order to pool their resources (financial, practical, material or symbolic), leading to the development of joint and consensual strategies to address issues in that place. They blend together the public, private and voluntary sectors. It is important, therefore, that they manipulate the perceptions of residents of the area to their common sense of good for the area.

To this end, therefore, any form of external agency (government, corporate body, community or local group) can seek to influence or create specific place-meanings, thereby shaping the actions and behaviours of individuals, groups, businesses and institutions. This is sometimes referred to as 're-imaging' and/or 'rebranding'.

Consider the example of Liverpool. Culture (popular music, the arts, sport) has dominated its recent rebranding. Liverpool has a rich history of popular music (notably The Beatles), and the performing and visual arts. It also has two Premier League football teams. Since 2003, when Liverpool was awarded the status of European Capital of Culture for 2008, the city centre has been transformed through major investment. In addition to the nearly £4 billion invested in regeneration, the city's economy is said to have been boosted by an annual £800 million of additional income. Over 15 million visitors were attracted to the city and the 7,000 cultural events it hosted in 2008. Attendance at the venues within the Albert Dock increased by over 30% and there were record visitor numbers across all of the city's attractions.

In some ways Liverpool's rebranding has made the city centre more similar to other city centres, but the city is still able to promote its distinctive cultural and maritime character. In recent years, up to 10 million tourists have visited Liverpool each year from the UK, other European countries and further afield, especially Japan and the USA. The budget airlines that use Liverpool's John Lennon Airport have boosted tourism to the city. In fact, these tourists have made Liverpool one of the ten most visited destinations in the UK. A variety of agencies have managed much of this increased popularity.

Place studies

This part of the specification requires you to understand two places through the collection, analysis and interpretation of quantitative and qualitative data, including their representation in the media.

Exam tip

Research one or more of these types of example and examine how the redevelopment partnerships manage the perception of place.

Knowledge check 21

Distinguish between rebranding, re-imaging and regeneration.

You must undertake two place studies:

1 Explore the developing character of a place local to your home or study centre.

2 Explore the developing character of a contrasting and distant place. This place could be in the same country or a different country but it must show significant contrast in terms of economic development and/or population density and/or cultural background and/or systems of political and economic organisation.

Both place studies must focus equally on **people's lived experience of the place in the past and at present**, and *either* **changing demographic and cultural characteristics** *or* **economic change and social inequalities**.

These place studies must apply the knowledge acquired through engagement with the specification content and demonstrate understanding of the ways in which your own life and those of others are affected by continuity and change in the nature of places.

Both place studies must use a variety of sources to acquire knowledge and understanding of the places and their changing characters. They must give particular weight to qualitative approaches involved in representing place, and to analysing critically the impacts of different media on place meanings and perceptions. You must also use quantitative data, including geospatial data, to present place characteristics. Their use should allow the development of critical perspectives on the data categories and approaches.

Suitable data sources could include:

■ statistics, such as census data
■ maps
■ geo-located data
■ geospatial data, including geographic information systems (GIS) applications
■ photographs
■ text, from varied media
■ audio-visual media
■ artistic representations
■ oral sources, such as interviews, reminiscence and songs

How do you assess the character of a place?

An obvious method of exploring the character of a place is by direct observation, especially the place local to you (note: as stated earlier, you should be thinking of a place you can walk around in 2 hours). Walk through the area, look at and simultaneously question what you see. Try to relate, interpret and assess your observations, i.e. form an opinion about 'what is good' and 'what is wrong', and map them.

While reading the environment you walk through, identify aspects you consider important to be changed (problems or issues) and those that are very characteristic of the place and should be maintained. It is important that you engage with the place on a personal level.

> **Exam tip**
>
> For your investigations, aim for a locality, neighbourhood or small community, either urban or rural. You should consider an area you can walk around in 2 hours.

You should also research further endogenous and exogenous information about the place, not acquired by your personal reading of its character, such as:

- physical morphology of the landscape
- history of the evolution of the place
- socioeconomic characteristics of the population of the area (possibly employing census data), including any people who may have come from overseas
- evidence and the dynamics of change in the area
- aspects of connectivity to the area, such as any transport systems
- how the area is featured in media, such as local newspapers

Your objective should be to get a comprehensive, interpretive and critical portrait of the place — a quick and meaningful sketch of the present situation and its dynamics towards change. Information can be mapped, labelled and illustrated (through photographs, sketches or verbal/video records) in order to describe, clearly and spatially, the results of your observations. You could use geospatial mechanisms and other forms of GIS.

Two or more people could also undertake direct observation of the character of the area. Multiplying the number of observers enriches the quality of the observation as long as they complete the task independently. By comparing and discussing results, you control, to some extent, deviation resulting from any individual subjectivity and observational weaknesses. You could ensure that you obtain updated maps and aerial photographs of the area (online platforms being very useful here), and start to collect cartography of the area produced over time, again possibly from online sources. This will show how the place has developed over time, and created its palimpsest.

Some themes to develop in the study of the historical evolution of the place could include:

- identification of the sequence of formation, filling and growth of the place
- development of its road layout
- details of significant events and agents in structuring the processes of this evolution
- evolution of the social fabric and ownership of the place, by its population and their activities
- the ages and types of buildings, and their state of preservation
- current building types, and ways in which they may be grouped or aggregated (e.g. housing types) by use or design
- historical and artistic ownership and/or representation, for example, in paintings and old photographs

Regarding the transport facilities in the place, you could identify:

- the main directions for public and private transport and any terminals/stops
- points of higher traffic intensity and possible conflict relating to the movement of cars, pedestrians and cyclists

Conducting interviews with people who know the area well (such as people connected with parish churches, health services, police officers and long-time inhabitants) is also important. All of these research methods will help you to formulate a mental map of the area.

Another interesting aspect of investigation concerns the presence of plant and animal species, through assessment of the proportion of the 'green' in relation to the 'built-up'. Vegetation surveys can take several different forms and involve varying functions, for example, gardens or public spaces, and can form part of the physical character that the place offers. You could consider the amount of open public space, and the degree to which landscaping has taken place.

Essentially, you are getting the place's 'portrait' at the time of observation.

Summary

After studying this topic, you should be able to:
- understand the nature and importance of place in human life and experiences
- appreciate the various perspectives and experiences of place
- explain how places develop meaning for their inhabitants, and evaluate the various ways in which places can be represented
- appreciate that a number of external agencies seek to manage and manipulate perceptions of place, mostly for positive reasons
- understand the factors that contribute to the developing character of places, some of which are endogenous and others exogenous
- analyse the forces that operate to change a place, and yet appreciate that all places have a context
- carry out two detailed studies of places at a local scale, as required by the specification

Questions & Answers

Assessment overview

In this section of the book, two sets of questions on each of the content areas are given: for Changing places there is one set of questions for AS and one for A-level, and for Global systems and global governance there are two sets of questions for A-level. For each of these, the style of questions used in the examination papers has been replicated, with a mixture of multiple-choice questions, short-answer questions, data-stimulus questions and extended-prose questions. Other than the multiple-choice questions and some short knowledge-based questions, all questions will be assessed using a 'levels of response' mark scheme to a maximum of four levels. The relative proportions and weightings of these questions varies between AS and A-level.

Each set of questions in this section is structured as follows:
- sample questions in the style of the examination
- mark schemes in the style of the examination
- example student answers at a variety of levels
- examiner's commentary on each of the above

For AS and A-level Geography, all assessments will test one or more of the following Assessment Objectives (AOs):
- **AO1:** Demonstrate knowledge and understanding of places, environments, concepts, processes, interactions and change, at a variety of scales.
- **AO2:** Apply knowledge and understanding in different contexts to interpret, analyse and evaluate geographical information and issues.
- **AO3:** Use a variety of relevant quantitative, qualitative and fieldwork skills to: investigate geographical questions and issues; interpret, analyse and evaluate data and evidence; construct arguments and draw conclusions.

All questions that carry a large number of marks (at AS and A-level) require students to consider connections between the subject matter and other aspects of geography, or develop deeper understanding, in order to access the highest marks. The former used to be referred to as synopticity, but the new term is **connections** — so try to think of **links** between the subject matter you are writing about and other areas of the specification. In some cases the required links will be indicated in the question.

For **AS** Changing places, 40 marks are available and the breakdown of questions is as follows:
- two 1-mark multiple-choice questions (AO1 or AO3)
- one 3-mark question (AO1)
- one 6-mark question with data — marked to two levels (AO3)
- one 9-mark question requiring extended-prose responses marked to three levels (AO1/AO2)
- one 20-mark question requiring extended-prose responses marked to four levels (AO1/AO2)

You should allocate *1 minute per mark* to answer the written questions.

For **A-level**, Global systems and global governance and Changing places are worth 36 marks each, and the breakdown of questions per topic is as follows:

- One 4-mark question (AO1)
- One 6-mark question with data — marked to two levels (AO3)
- One 6-mark question with data — marked to two levels (AO1/AO2)
- One 20-mark question requiring extended-prose responses — marked to four levels (AO1/AO2)

You should allocate *1½ minutes per mark* to answer the written questions.

For each sample question below, two answers have been provided: one at the upper end of the mark range, and the other at a mid-level. Study carefully the descriptions of the 'levels' given in the mark schemes and understand the requirements (or 'triggers') necessary to move an answer from one level to the one above it. You should also read the commentary with the mark schemes to understand why credit has or has not been awarded. For the weaker answers, the commentary highlights areas for improvement, specific problems and common errors, such as lack of clarity, weak development, lack of examples, irrelevance, misinterpretation and mistaken meanings of terms. In all cases, actual marks are indicated.

The extended-response writing tasks at both AS and A-level, which each carry 20 marks, will be assessed using a generic mark scheme such as the one shown below. Study this carefully to see what is needed to move from one level to the next.

Note: AS questions are not available for Global systems and global governance.

Level/mark range	Criteria/descriptor
Level 4 (16–20 marks)	■ Detailed evaluative conclusion that is rational and firmly based on knowledge and understanding which is applied to the context of the question (AO2). ■ Detailed, coherent and relevant analysis and evaluation in the application of knowledge and understanding throughout (AO2). ■ Full evidence of links between knowledge and understanding to the application of knowledge and understanding in different contexts (AO2). ■ Detailed, highly relevant and appropriate knowledge and understanding of place(s) and environments used throughout (AO1). ■ Full and accurate knowledge and understanding of key concepts and processes throughout (AO1). ■ Detailed awareness of scale and temporal change, which is well integrated where appropriate (AO1).
Level 3 (11–15 marks)	■ Clear evaluative conclusion that is based on knowledge and understanding, which is applied to the context of the question (AO2). ■ Generally clear, coherent and relevant analysis and evaluation in the application of knowledge and understanding (AO2). ■ Generally clear evidence of links between knowledge and understanding to the application of knowledge and understanding in different contexts (AO2). ■ Generally clear and relevant knowledge and understanding of place(s) and environments (AO1). ■ Generally clear and accurate knowledge and understanding of key concepts and processes (AO1). ■ Generally clear awareness of scale and temporal change, which is integrated where appropriate (AO1).

Level/mark range	Criteria/descriptor
Level 2 (6–10 marks)	■ Some sense of an evaluative conclusion partially based upon knowledge and understanding, which is applied to the context of the question (AO2). ■ Some partially relevant analysis and evaluation in the application of knowledge and understanding (AO2). ■ Some evidence of links between knowledge and understanding to the application of knowledge and understanding in different contexts (AO2). ■ Some relevant knowledge and understanding of place(s) and environments, which is partially relevant (AO1). ■ Some knowledge and understanding of key concepts and processes (AO1). ■ Some awareness of scale and temporal change, which is sometimes integrated where appropriate. There may be a few inaccuracies (AO1).
Level 1 (1–5 marks)	■ Very limited and/or unsupported evaluative conclusion that is loosely based upon knowledge and understanding, which is applied to the context of the question (AO2). ■ Very limited analysis and evaluation in the application of knowledge and understanding. This lacks clarity and coherence (AO2). ■ Very limited and rarely logical evidence of links between knowledge and understanding to the application of knowledge and understanding in different contexts (AO2). ■ Very limited relevant knowledge and understanding of place(s) and environments (AO1). ■ Isolated knowledge and understanding of key concepts and processes. ■ Very limited awareness of scale and temporal change, which is rarely integrated where appropriate. There may be a number of inaccuracies (AO1).
Level 0 (0 marks)	■ Nothing worthy of credit.

Examination skills

Command words used in the examinations

Command words are the words and phrases used in exams and other assessment tasks that tell students how they should answer the question. The following command words could be used:

Analyse Break down concepts, information and/or issues to convey an understanding of them by finding connections and causes, and/or effects.

Annotate Add to a diagram, image or graphic a number of words that describe and/or explain features, rather than just identify them (which is labelling).

Assess Consider several options or arguments and weigh them up so as to come to a conclusion about their effectiveness or validity.

Comment on Make a statement that arises from a factual point made — add a view, or an opinion, or an interpretation. In data/stimulus response questions, examine the stimulus material provided and then make statements about the material and its content that are relevant, appropriate and geographical, but not directly evident.

Compare Describe the similarities and differences between at least two phenomena.

Contrast Point out the differences between at least two phenomena.

Critically Often occurs before 'assess' or 'evaluate', inviting an examination of an issue from the point of view of a critic with a particular focus on the strengths and weaknesses of the points of view being expressed.

Define/What is meant by State the precise meaning of an idea or concept.

Describe Give an account in words of a phenomenon that may be an entity, an event, a feature, a pattern, a distribution or a process. For example, if describing a landform, say what it looks like, give some indication of size or scale, what it is made of and where it is in relation to something else (field relationship).

Discuss Set out both sides of an argument (for and against), and come to a conclusion related to the content and emphasis of the discussion. There should be some evidence of balance, although not necessarily of equal weighting.

Distinguish between Give the meaning of two (or more) phenomena and make it clear how they are different from each other.

Evaluate Consider several options, ideas or arguments and form a view based on evidence about their importance/validity/merit/utility.

Examine Consider carefully and provide a detailed account of the indicated topic.

Explain/Why/Suggest reasons for Set out the causes of a phenomenon and/or the factors that influence its form/nature. This usually requires an understanding of processes.

Interpret Ascribe meaning to geographical information and issues.

Justify Give reasons for the validity of a view or idea or why some action should be undertaken. This might reasonably involve discussing and discounting alternative views or actions.

Outline/Summarise Provide a brief account of relevant information.

To what extent Form and express a view as to the merit or validity of a view or statement after examining the evidence available and/or different sides of an argument.

■ AS questions

Changing places

Examples of multiple-choice questions

Question 1

Representation of place refers to: (1 mark)

A the meaning that serves to create and/or maintain relationships within a place

B the cultural practices by which human societies interpret and portray the world around them

C the broader context of a place comprising the built and social environment

D the way in which places are described in the media and by the written word

Question 2

Which of the following statements is correct? (1 mark)

A Census data provide a useful background to the character of the population of an area.

B Census data are an up-to-date form of quantitative data.

C Qualitative data, such as interviews with people, are more reliable than census data.

D Census data are not useful as they are always out of date.

Study Table 1, which shows census data from two cities in England, and answer the questions below.

Table 1 Census data on two places: City A and City B, population by age group, 2011 (%)

Age	City A	City B	England
0–4	7.4	5.6	6.3
5–9	6.3	4.2	5.6
10–14	6.1	4.6	5.8
15–19	7.4	6.1	6.3
20–24	10.7	9.3	6.8
25–29	9.0	8.1	6.9
30–44*	20.7	21.3	20.6
45–59*	16.9	17.4	19.4
60–64	4.3	5.6	6.0
65–74*	5.7	8.0	8.6
75–84*	3.9	6.3	5.5
85–89	1.1	2.1	1.5
90 and over*	0.5	1.3	0.8
Total population	**329,839**	**183,491**	**53,012,456**

Source: ONS

* Note: the figures for these age groups were not published as five-year cohorts like the rest of the data. The figures may not add up to 100% because of rounding.

Question 3

Which of the following statements is correct? (1 mark)

A In City A and City B there are more people between 30 and 34 than in any other age group.

B City B has a higher proportion of retired people than England as a whole.

C City B has a more youthful population than City A.

D Over 2/5 of the population in England is between the ages of 30 and 59.

Question 4

Which of the following statements is correct? (1 mark)

A   The dependency ratio of England is lower than both cities.

B   City A has a much higher dependency ratio.

C   City B has a much higher dependency ratio.

D   The dependency ratios of both cities are very similar.

Question 5

Which of the following statements is correct? (1 mark)

A   In City A the death rate is increasing.

B   In City A there is a high proportion of people working after retirement.

C   City A has a lower proportion of people over 65 than City B.

D   City B has more people living to over 100 than England as a whole.

Answers to multiple-choice questions

Question 1

Correct answer B. (1 mark)

Question 2

Correct answer A. (1 mark)

Question 3

Correct answer B. (1 mark)

Question 4

Correct answer D. (1 mark)

Questions 5

Correct answer C. (1 mark)

Written answer questions

Question 1

Outline how you can investigate a place using qualitative data. (3 marks)

ⓔ **Mark scheme: 1 mark per valid point.**

> **Student A**
>
> I can use qualitative data such as photographs, text, from varied media, audio-visual media, artistic representations and oral sources, such as interviews, reminiscences, songs, etc. **a** Most people now have digital cameras on their mobile phones, which can use wide-angle and close-up shots. **b** These can be used to monitor changes over time. Conducting interviews with people can be useful in finding out how a person feels about a place **c**, and their changing emotions as there has been both continuity and change in that community **d**.

ⓔ **3/3 marks awarded. a–c** Student A provides three valid statements. **d** Note how the student qualifies a point in the final sentence to gain 2 marks in the sentence, if they were available. Maximum credit has already been awarded.

> **Student B**
>
> Qualitative data are comments by people who live in or may visit a place. **a** These things would need to be investigated by questionnaires with open questions or by interviews. **b** Another form of qualitative data is how places are recorded or judged in various forms of media such as songs and poems. **c** It gives a sense of place.

ⓔ **3/3 marks awarded. a–c** Student B also provides three valid statements.

Question 2

Figure 1 shows two photographs of contrasting places in which a religious building is central to the community. Compare the character of the places shown. (6 marks)

a   b

Figure 1 Contrasting places in which a religious building is central to the community

ⓔ Mark scheme:

■ **Level 2 (4–6 marks): Clear interpretation and comparison of the information shown in the photographs with some qualification that makes appropriate use of data to support. Interpretation may have some detail and/or sophistication.**

■ **Level 1 (1–3 marks): Basic interpretation and comparison of the information shown in the photographs, with limited use of data to support.**

Student A

Photo B is of a village in the UK with a church with a tower, though it has several steeples on the tower. On the other hand Photo A shows a mosque somewhere in a developing country. a The mosque has a gold dome on it, and this would suggest that it has some very rich mosque-goers. On the other hand the UK church is composed of stone and looks much older than the mosque. It may be medieval in age. b

In the foreground of Photo B there are cars parked in what appears to be a school playground, whereas in Photo A there are shanty-town houses on stilts in the water c, which makes me suggest that it is a developing country. There is a small boat and there is no sign of any cars d.

ⓔ **2/6 marks awarded.** a c d Student A provides a number of straightforward comparisons by simply stating what can be seen and linking them. b The commentary that follows is also fairly simple and unsophisticated. The answer is typical of a mid-Level 1 answer.

Student B

Religious buildings are often at the centre of communities around the world. They are one of the endogenous features that help to determine the character of places. ⓐ In the case of Photo A, there is a large modern mosque in the midst of some fairly dull concrete buildings in the background and a stilted house community in the foreground. Despite a sense of generally lower overall income in the community, the mosque itself has one very large and a number of smaller gold-covered domes. This is a sign that much of the wealth in the community has been invested in this building. The same would have been the case when the church in Photo B was constructed, possibly in Victorian times or earlier. For a village community to have built such an ornate tower in those days would have meant that some rich landowner would have donated money, possibly seeking his salvation at his death. This was culturally very important in those days. ⓑ

The areas around the religious buildings show quite large contrasts. In Photo B there appears to be a village school with some cars parked in the playground. Small schools in village such as this will have a number of mixed-age classes, but all children in the village will be able to attend. The foreground of Photo A is much more typical of a developing world city where poor people have to find a cheap place to live — in this case, in stilted houses with corrugated iron roofs over a river or coastline. One wonders if all the children here go to a school that is free. The contrast in wealth here is quite stark. ⓒ

ⓔ **6/6 marks awarded.** Bearing in mind that there are only 8 minutes to consider these photographs and answer the question, the opening statements are very sophisticated. ⓐ Student B has fully understood the phrase 'character of the places' and applied some theoretical aspects at the outset. ⓑ The remainder of the first paragraph shows evidence of maturity of thought and depth of knowledge and understanding. ⓒ The second paragraph is not as strong but the student does attempt to make a comparison with some commentary. High Level 2 awarded.

Question 3

Evaluate how external agencies, such as governments, corporate bodies and community groups, attempt to influence or create place-meanings. (9 marks)

ⓔ Mark scheme:

■ Level 3 (7–9 marks):

  ☐ AO1: demonstrates detailed knowledge and understanding of concepts, processes, interactions and change. These underpin the response throughout.

  ☐ AO2: applies knowledge and understanding appropriately and with detail. Detailed evidence of the drawing together of a range of geographical ideas, which is used constructively to support the response. Evaluation is detailed and well supported with appropriate evidence. A well-balanced and coherent argument is presented.

- Level 2 (4–6 marks):
  - ☐ AO1: demonstrates some appropriate knowledge and understanding of concepts, processes, interactions and change. These are mostly relevant although there may be some minor inaccuracy.
  - ☐ AO2: applies some knowledge and understanding appropriately. Emerging evidence of the drawing together of a range of geographical ideas, which is used to support the response. Evaluation is clear with some support of evidence. A clear argument is presented.
- Level 1 (1–3 marks):
  - ☐ AO1: demonstrates basic/limited knowledge and understanding of concepts, processes, interactions and change. These offer limited relevance and/or there is some inaccuracy.
  - ☐ AO2: applies limited knowledge and understanding appropriately. Basic evidence of drawing together of a range of geographical ideas, which is used at a basic level to support the response. Evaluation is basic with limited support of evidence. A basic argument is presented.

Student A

Local governments often try to influence and manage perceptions of places, especially when trying to seek inward investment into their areas. In 2015, the North East Lincolnshire Council, a local government body, announced that a major redevelopment scheme would hopefully take place in Grimsby, a town on the North Sea coast of England. As part of their publicity material, they produced a page on their website that attempted to manage the perception of the area about to undergo redevelopment.

The language used on the website page referred to plans to help 'transform' Grimsby into a 'more vibrant and attractive place'. a The council also prepared a new Local Plan, which suggested how the borough might grow and develop in the future. The Local Plan focused on three core themes: jobs, homes and places, and recognised the need to improve the quality of life, particularly for disadvantaged people, support the growth of the local economy, protect the environment and build new homes.

In terms of supporting the growth of the local economy, the council proposed discussion on the growth of the offshore renewables industry and the opportunities this presents for North East Lincolnshire. It stated that the town was 'fortunate' to enjoy a location at the mouth of the Humber and North Sea, which presented 'a worldwide gateway' for trade and business. b It stressed that this would provide new opportunities in the offshore wind sector as well as further growth in other sectors such as seafood, ports and logistics, energy and chemicals. The council stated that the challenge would be to 'capture this potential' c, and it hoped that the Local Plan would help achieve it by building a stronger economy and stronger communities in the town.

The council also made use of a strong visual image, an artistic impression of one new building in the redevelopment. d It is clear, therefore, that the council is seeking to put forward a positive view of the town and counter any negative views that people both within and beyond the town may have about investing or even living in it. They are obviously trying to manage perceptions of the town both within and beyond in a very positive sense.

ⓔ **8/9 marks awarded.** The answer makes good use of a detailed case study that has clearly been studied in class or at home. **a–c** Student A selects extracts from a website aimed at raising the perceptions of the town of Grimsby and uses these to good effect. There is a strong sense of evaluation throughout, which enables the answer to access Level 3. **d** The only disappointing aspect is the reference to a visual image, which is not developed. Mid Level 3 awarded.

Student B

Sometimes community groups can try to influence or create new place meanings and add to the character that a place already has. This can sometimes occur for small rural towns that might appear to be off the beaten track but need to find a way to rediscover themselves. In these cases, it can be the local shopkeepers who are keen to unite and raise the perception of the town. **a**

Ludlow in Shropshire was the first UK town to join an Italian movement called Cittaslow. The Cittaslow manifesto was drawn up by the movement's founders, a group of mayors from Italian towns. It says: 'We are looking for towns brought to life by people who make time to enjoy a quality of life'. They focus on towns that have a number of public spaces, theatres, shops, cafés, inns and historic buildings. They also want towns where traditional craft skills are in use, and where there is the availability of local agricultural produce, in season. The manifesto wants to unite towns where healthy eating, healthy living and enjoying life are central to the community. Finally, they want to slow down the pace of life in the town and enjoy what it has to offer.

Ludlow has had a summer festival since the 1960s featuring concerts and outdoor Shakespeare plays in the castle grounds. Also since the 1990s, the Ludlow Festival of Food and Drink has taken place every September. Over 150 small local food producers showcase and sell their goods in and around the castle. The three-day event involves food and drink trails, including the famous 'sausage trail', on which participants walk between butchers' shops and sample different sausages before voting on their favourite. There is also a smaller Christmas food festival held in November. The town has become proud of its tradition of high-quality, locally produced food and still has a number of traditional butchers and bakers, a farmers' market and a range of specialist food shops. **b** The perception of Ludlow is therefore one of a healthy eating and fun place to visit.

ⓔ **6/9 marks awarded. a** Student B begins with a good introduction that explains why some community groups seek to influence place-meanings. The following case study of Ludlow is now in context. **b** Unfortunately, what follows is a detailed account of the methods by which shopkeepers in Ludlow have sought to influence the perception of Ludlow, but with little analysis or evaluation of success — note the word 'how' in the question. What evaluation is provided is mainly implicit rather than explicit. There is detailed material in here but it needs to be used more effectively to answer the question set. High Level 2 awarded.

Question 4

Evaluate how well places may be represented in a variety of different forms. (20 marks)

(e) Mark scheme: see the generic extended-response mark scheme in the table on pages 48–49.

> ## Student A
>
> Today's towns and cities face numerous challenges. The 'high street' in its various forms has always been a good indicator of how well a city is doing. Empty shops and the wrong retail mix create a bad impression of a city's health — a poor representation. There are other historical factors that have led to the decline of many cities and they can be linked to economic changes brought about by deindustrialisation and decline in recent decades. For many town centres, such as in Rotherham and Hull, there has been a continued labelling of decline and lack of social cohesion, not helped by the recent controversies regarding child sexual abuse in the former. a
>
> A key to the revival of cities as a whole is the vitality of city centres, and this is crucial to how they are perceived. Many cities have had to adapt to survive, and their city centres have acted as engines of the new economy. Places such as Birmingham, the Docklands and parts of Manchester have become adopters of this new wave of change, seeking to improve their image. Local authority partnerships and increasingly private companies such as Urban Splash have played their part. Nowadays planners and architects attempt to create positive urban change through retail, leisure, culture and science. Several cities, such as Liverpool, have tried to raise their 'cultural offer' especially as it links strongly with a 'place aspiration' of high-quality city living. So, successful re-imaging through good advertising could combine 'place representation' with high-quality accommodation and world-class services. b
>
> One recent example is that of the promotional material for Hull 2017 UK City of Culture. c Its message is one of 'a city finding its place in the UK, a city coming out of the shadows and re-establishing its reputation as a gateway that welcomes the world'. Hull is a city that faces challenges in terms of employment, educational attainment and external perceptions in the media that have often been negative. The awarding of City of Culture could therefore act as an important catalyst for Hull. The organisers estimate that there will be a £60 million boost to the local economy in 2017 alone. There are already early economic benefits, with the city experiencing a 29% increase in Trip Advisor visits (a form of representation in tourist agency material) and a 54% increase in museum visits (another form of cultural representation) during holiday periods.
>
> Hull is determined that the City of Culture 2017 will leave a lasting legacy through the development of visitor priority areas like the old town, fruit market and waterfront. However, the isolated geography of the city is another consideration. The city has one main rail line in and out of it, and is at the end of the M62 motorway. The process of re-imaging, and modifying its representation, by attracting a wider audience and economic base is therefore challenging for the city. d

ⓔ 14/20 marks awarded. This is a conceptually strong answer that begins with a background as to how urban areas can be represented either in people's perceptions or in general forms of advertising. **ⓐ ⓑ** The first two paragraphs deal with these conceptual points, but the former introduces some wider discussion of contemporary social issues — useful links to other parts of the specification. However, the theme of representation is only fleetingly referred to, almost as an afterthought. The following two paragraphs are better and make good use of support material — the case study is a good one to select as it illustrates how 'representation' is a key element of Hull's re-imaging. **ⓒ** The response is dominated by one form of representation — the role of promotional material — although there are references to other forms. There is a clear sense of evaluation throughout, although perhaps not as explicit as it could be. **ⓓ** The final section assesses the potential success of Hull's City of Culture bid rather than the representation of it. There is some good material here, and it merits Level 3 overall, but not at the top of the level. Mid Level 3 awarded.

Student B

Croyde is a small seaside village on the north Devon coast. In postcards of the area, it is often represented as a village surrounded by spectacular landscapes with idyllic cliffs and seaside cottages, surfing waves, gorse and even ponies. It looks and sounds a wonderful place. However, all is not how it seems. **ⓐ**

Like many rural communities throughout the UK, Croyde's agricultural economy has suffered in recent years. The epidemic of mad cow disease of the late 1990s, followed by the foot and mouth outbreak that began in 2001, both damaged farming in the area. **ⓑ** The population under the age of 16 is low compared with the rest of the UK and the percentage above retirement age is high. Employment opportunities beyond the primary sector are limited and this has led to significant out-migration of young working populations to urban areas. There has been a loss of community spirit and of artisanal agricultural practices. **ⓒ**

In an effort to reduce the loss of young people from the area and to stimulate economic growth, surfing is being used as a re-imaging tool and as a means of diversifying the economy. Croyde has set itself up as one of southwest England's premium locations for surfing, with a dedicated website. Throughout the summer the beach and village centre buzz with surfers and the amenities they require. The peak of activity comes with Croyde's Gold Coast Oceanfest, which combines surfing and music and is held annually in mid-June. **ⓓ** The village is therefore changing the way in which it is recognised and represented.

The key players in bringing about this re-imaging strategy are made up of a mixture of public organisations and private investors. Local farmers have converted buildings into bed and breakfast accommodation and turned fields into caravan parks. The North Devon District Council has supported developments by granting planning permissions that have allowed surfing amenities to develop. The local parish council has set up the Deckchair Cinema, which is held in the village hall. **ⓔ**

The example of Croyde illustrates well the way that advertising involving the written word and selective use of photographic imagery, aided by technology, seeks to provide a different perspective on a place. In this case, the former experiences of the area for some people do not strictly match the new representations made. For the time being, surfing has been successfully used as a re-imaging tool in Croyde. We must hope that it does not jeopardise the rural charm, which provides the village with an initial, unique selling point. [i]

(e) **20/20 marks awarded.** [a] This answer is more focused on the task, and addresses the theme of representation more directly, and at the outset in the first paragraph. [b] The following paragraph explains why another form of representation of the village of Croyde was necessary, with an interesting contextual linkage point into farming practices, and [c] further material linked with population and migration. [d] The reasons for the changing representation of the village are then provided in the next paragraph. [e] There is a logical flow to the argument here. The role of differing agents in the changes is illustrated well. [i] Finally, the conclusion brings the themes of representation and evaluation to the forefront. This is a well-worked, coherent response. Maximum marks awarded.

■ A-level questions

Global systems and global governance

Set of questions A

Question 1

Summarise the main features of international trade. (4 marks)

(e) **Mark scheme: 1 mark per valid point.**

> **Student A**
>
> World trade is dominated by China and the OECD countries (USA, countries of the EU, Australia, Japan, Canada, Switzerland, Mexico, South Korea, etc.), and much of the trade is between these countries. [a] These are mainly economically advanced states and much of the trade is in manufactured goods. [b] However, as other countries such as Brazil and India have begun to industrialise, they have tended to progress from industries which are 'export-oriented', such as basic processing of raw materials, to those which are 'import substitution', such as the manufacture of textiles, clothing, shoes, cigarettes and drinks. [c] In 2013, China became the world's biggest trader in goods, with imports and exports totalling over US$4 trillion. [d]

(e) **4/4 marks awarded.** [a]–[d] Student A provides four valid statements.

Student B

Much of world trade is dominated by the large industrial countries of the USA, Europe and China. **a** Most of this trade is in the form of manufactured goods and is transported by ships carrying huge numbers of containers. **b** There is also a large trade in oil and natural gas, again by tankers from areas such as the Middle East, with the country of Saudi Arabia being a dominant exporter. **c**

e **3/4 marks awarded. a–c** Student B provides three valid statements.

Question 2

Figure 2 shows the ratios of the volume of commodity imports against exports (commodity dependency) for countries around the world. Interpret the information shown.   (6 marks)

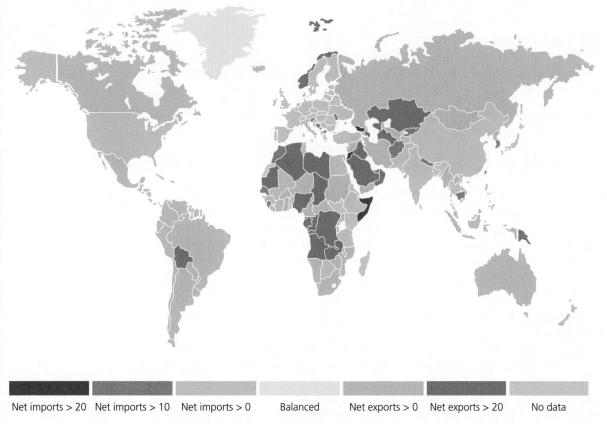

Net imports > 20   Net imports > 10   Net imports > 0   Balanced   Net exports > 0   Net exports > 20   No data

Figure 2 Commodity (oils, metals and food) dependency 2014 (%)

ⓔ Mark scheme:

■ Level 2 (4–6 marks): clear interpretation of the data shown in the map with some qualification and/or quantification that makes appropriate use of data to support. Interpretation may have some detail and/or sophistication.

■ Level 1 (1–3 marks): basic interpretation of the data shown in the map (likely to be largely highs and lows), with limited use of data to support.

Student A

The map shows the degree to which there is trade dependency of commodities such as oil, metals and food, i.e. how much the volume of exports outweighs imports and vice versa, for all the countries in the world. ⓐ Some countries, such as those in Central Africa, North Africa and Central Asia, show a high relationship of exports to imports, over 20%. This means that they export more than they import. This will mean that if the demand for their exports falls, then they will be in difficulty as they have surplus products to sell. ⓑ

On the other hand, there are countries such as the USA, most of Europe, India and China that import much more by volume than they export. This could mean that they have a trade deficit and therefore they will be in debt. ⓒ Many countries in Europe, for example, have a trade deficit, which means they either lose money or have to make it up by providing services. ⓓ

This should mean that the first group of countries I mentioned will be rich, if they export more than they import. But this depends on the nature of the commodity they are exporting, as Saudi Arabia exports a lot of oil and so is wealthy. ⓔ

ⓔ **4/6 marks awarded.** ⓐ Initially, Student A provides a basic attempt at the question, and wastes a little time by explaining what the map shows — this is not necessary. A series of straightforward and simple statements is then made, ⓑ one about the high export/import countries, and then ⓒ the high import/export countries. ⓓ The latter does, however, have a slightly more sophisticated statement. ⓔ This level of interpretation is also repeated in the last sentence. Low Level 2 awarded.

Student B

The first thing to notice in the figure is the degree to which there are variations in trade dependency of commodities around the world. ⓐ Some countries of the world that export commodities such as oil — those in the Middle East, for example — have huge positive balances, over 20%. This means that they are accumulating huge amounts of revenue from selling their commodity, oil. ⓑ The positive percentage is also high in some central African countries too, but the amount of wealth generated may vary as not all are exporting oil. Angola and Nigeria are, but the Republic of the Congo is not — it exports metals. ⓒ Whatever the commodity being exported, it may mean that they make a lot of money when the commodity is in demand, but when the demand falls, or the price of it falls on the world market, then their income may dry up quickly. These countries are at the whim of the world's stock markets. ⓓ

At the other end of the spectrum are countries such as the USA and most of Europe, and even China and India, which import more commodities of oil, metals and food than they export. Most of these countries are developed countries that will have greater exports of manufactured goods and/or services and therefore are not at risk of price fluctuations. Countries such as India and China now rely on imports of commodities to fuel their rapid economic growth, similar to the countries of Western Europe in the past.

ⓔ 6/6 marks awarded. ⓐ Student B makes a perceptive opening statement, which demonstrates that he/she has spent some time looking at the data before putting pen to paper. **ⓑ–ⓔ** From then on, a series of statements is made that combine descriptive statements from the data together with valid interpretation that show both knowledge and understanding. Maximum mark within Level 2 awarded.

Question 3

Figure 3 provides information about inequality in the world. Evaluate the degree to which inequality exists in the world.

(6 marks)

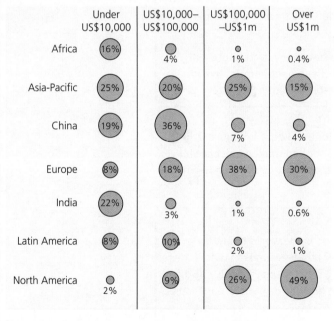

Source: Credit Suisse Global Wealth Databook 2015

Figure 3 Global wealth distribution among adults, by region (2015)

ⓔ Mark scheme:

■ **Level 2 (4–6 marks):**

☐ AO1: demonstrates clear knowledge and understanding of concepts, processes, interactions and change.

☐ AO2: applies knowledge and understanding to the novel situation, offering clear analysis and evaluation drawn appropriately from the context provided. Clear statements of 'degree to which'.

■ **Level 1 (1–3 marks):**

   ☐ **AO1:** demonstrates basic knowledge and understanding of concepts, processes, interactions and change.

   ☐ **AO2:** applies limited knowledge and understanding to the novel situation, offering basic analysis and evaluation drawn from the context provided. Tentative or no statement of 'degree to which'.

Student A

Figure 3 shows the huge disparity of wealth that exists in the world today. If we take the extremes, almost half of the adult population in the USA has over US$1 million in wealth, whereas in Africa, India and Latin America, 1% or less have that amount of money. **a** In Asia-Pacific and India over 20% of the population have less than US$10,000 in wealth. **b** Of course, much of this perceived wealth will be taken up by housing and personal possessions, such as cars. Many people in the USA own large houses — sometimes referred to as 'real estate'. On the other hand people in India and Asia-Pacific will not own their own homes, and the majority of houses will be in a poor state of repair.

The Asia-Pacific region is quite unusual in that there is roughly a similar proportion in each of the four categories of wealth, whereas in Europe over two-thirds of the adult population has a wealth of US$100,000 or more. **c** Hence there is great inequality within this region.

It is fair to say that Africa, India and Latin America have very few people with high incomes, say over US$100,000. **d** This means these people must live in other parts of the world, and so there must be great inequality. **e**

---

e **2/6 marks awarded.** Student A has misunderstood the data in Figure 3. **a–c** There are several incorrect statements. **d** The final section makes one correct statement based on the data, followed by **e** a weak statement of 'degree to which'. Mid Level 1 awarded.

Student B

Figure 3 shows that there is a great disparity of wealth in the world today. If we take the highest level of wealth — over $1 million per adult — almost a half of these people live in the USA, with another third in Europe. **a** This means that only one-fifth of the world's richest people live somewhere else in the world. **b** The proportions in India and Africa are tiny. **c** At the other extreme, 66% of the world's poorest people, with less than US$10,000 to their name, live in some part of Asia, with two-thirds of them being in China and India. **d** These two statistics taken together indicate that there is massive disparity of wealth and inequality in the world. **e**

However, not all is doom and gloom, as there are signs that some wealth is being spread to other parts of the world. For example, over a third of those people with between US$10,000 and US$100,000 live in China. This must be a sign that wealth is beginning to spread here — the proportion is similar to that of the Chinese population in the world. This indicates that the massive industrial development that has taken place here is being reflected in personal incomes. **f**

Interestingly, India is also going through a period of industrial growth, more so in services. However, the proportions of people in those wealth groups of over US$10,000 are all small, and much smaller than the proportion of the Indian population compared with the world. This would indicate that wealth generation is not happening in India, and that internal wealth disparity and inequality must be large here. g

e **6/6 marks awarded.** Student B demonstrates clear understanding of the data, in that they show proportions of various wealth categories in different parts of the world. a–d The first paragraph includes a number of correct qualitative comments based on the data. Note how the student does not repeat the data, but shows some evidence of processing of it. e This is then followed by a clear statement of 'degree to which'. f The second paragraph continues this strategy but also makes use of wider knowledge and understanding of the possible reasons behind the data for China. g The answer ends with a strong sense of evaluation and commentary regarding the apparent anomaly of India. All elements of Level 2 have been addressed — full marks awarded.

Question 4

Evaluate the degree to which sustainability is possible when it comes to managing the global commons of Antarctica and the seas around it. (20 marks)

e **Mark scheme: see the generic extended-response mark scheme in the table on pages 48–49.**

Student A

Antarctica and the seas around it are unusual global commons. Unlike the others, Antarctica is locked in a longstanding territorial dispute. Seven states — Argentina, Australia, Chile, France, New Zealand, Norway and the UK — believe that parts of the polar continent and the sea around it fall under their national jurisdiction. Two other states — Russia and the USA — have reserved the right to make their own claims in the future. Every other member of the international community rejects these claims. The Antarctic Treaty has, for now, been used to manage these disagreements over the ownership of Antarctica. a

The Antarctic Treaty was negotiated in Washington, DC in 1959. Twelve states agreed to a treaty designed to manage the dispute over the ownership of the polar continent. The negotiating parties pledged to work together peacefully, using science and international cooperation, and put to one side the disputes over jurisdiction and ownership.

Antarctica was demilitarised, and a system of inspection was instituted to ensure compliance and goodwill. The Treaty has been successful. The region remains a zone of peace. The parties manage resource sustainability issues such as fishing, and continue to accommodate new members, from Brazil, China and India to, most recently, Pakistan and Mongolia. b

Despite the Antarctic Treaty, the region faces a series of profound challenges regarding sustainability. These vary in scope and intensity from the impacts of ongoing climate change, to managing issues such as fishing, whaling, scientific activity, mineral exploitation, biological prospecting and tourism. All these activities are managed in a legal no-man's land, where national and international rules and regulations criss-cross the polar continent and Southern Ocean. c Two examples are examined here.

Fishing, sealing and whaling have been longstanding features of the human relationship with Antarctica. Over-exploitation of these resources has led to good examples of poor sustainability, and has been called 'the tragedy of the commons'. Seal and whale stocks were devastated in the nineteenth and twentieth centuries. As commercial whaling declined in the 1960s distant-water fishing vessels became more prevalent in the Southern Ocean. The Convention for the Conservation of Antarctic Marine Living Resources (CCAMLR), negotiated by Antarctic Treaty parties in the late 1970s, was a world leader in terms of fisheries management. It used fisheries science to establish quotas (total allowable catches) and create a complex zonation of the Southern Ocean, in an attempt to create sustainability. However, in the last 20 years the system has come under greater pressure. Illegal, unregulated and unreported fishing remains a problem. Some members, in particular China, Spain, Korea and Russia, are pushing for greater resource exploitation rather than conservation. Others (e.g. Australia and New Zealand) are suspected of using recent proposals for extended marine protected areas (MPAs) to consolidate their sovereign interests in the Southern Ocean. Japan and Australia have been locked in a bitter legal dispute over the future of 'scientific whaling' in the Southern Ocean to the south of Australia. Although it is managed by the International Whaling Commission, whaling is deeply divisive and Japan has rejected Australian claims that there is an Australian whaling sanctuary just off the Australian Antarctic Territory. d

The Antarctic Treaty deliberately omitted any reference to Antarctic mineral potential, for fear it would jeopardise the agreement. In 1991 the Protocol on Environmental Protection was negotiated, and this entered into force in 1998, prohibiting all forms of mineral exploitation. However, this ban can be revisited in the year 2048. In the last decade, there have been signs that some countries want to revisit the mineral question. China and Russia, in particular, have been accused of consolidating their presence on the Antarctic continent (in the form of scientific stations) for the purpose of strengthening their interest in long-term mineral wealth. e

The resource potential of the Antarctic is already being exploited through biological prospecting. This involves taking Antarctic life forms and converting them for commercial use, for example, using Antarctic green algae in skin cosmetics. This is approved activity, but the commercialisation of Antarctica's resources clearly places pressures on maintaining sustainability in the region. f Biological prospecting may offer an insight into the tensions that may arise if resources such as oil, gas, iron ore, zinc, lead and coal were to be exploited.

The Antarctic, and the sea around it, is a contested global commons. The Antarctic Treaty imposes some regulations but it does not work in isolation. Seven states believe that they own a part of Antarctica (and one part remains unclaimed). Other international frameworks and regional agreements on biodiversity, fisheries management, whaling and climate change have relevance for the future of a sustainable Antarctica. g

🅔 **18/20 marks awarded.** a Student A begins with an interesting introduction, pointing out that the current management of Antarctica is fraught with difficulty. This sets the scene of evaluation well. b The following paragraph provides more detail on the Antarctic Treaty (the management), again with a sense of evaluation. c The fourth paragraph then provides some context for the sustainability issues to be introduced later. d A highly detailed paragraph on the sustainability issues regarding fishing and whaling follows, with a sense of evaluation being clear, for example: 'the tragedy of the commons', 'the system has come under greater pressure' and 'remains a problem'. e The following paragraph is less detailed, but raises the issue of mineral extraction. f This is followed by an interesting section concerning the use of algae for cosmetics, which seemingly is an approved activity. g The answer ends with a weak conclusion that does not fully address the question. This is a pity, as the preceding material is excellent. Mid Level 4 awarded.

Student B

In the Southern Ocean in the early 1800s whaling and fishing were a big problem as by 1980 there were very few seals and whales left as they were farmed for their oil and bones. However, by 1998 this was regulated and now this can only be done for scientific research, which many countries say they do, like Norway and Japan. They are only allowed to fish for around 100 whales a year as, due to the cold climate, the replacement rate is low, making this much more sustainable than before, as 5,000 seals and whales were dying each year and now only around 75 die in one year. a

However, over-fishing and whaling continue to be major threats to the region. Illegal, unregulated and unreported fishing in the Southern Ocean threatens fish stocks and the seabirds and marine mammals that depend upon them. This is not a sustainable situation for the ecology of the area and the complex food webs that exist. There is careful monitoring of krill, which is the staple of the marine ecosystem and if overfished has implications for the whole food chain, too. b

Fishing in the Southern Ocean has had to be regulated and controlled to prevent overfishing and exploitation. Limits have been set on the amount of fish taken from the Southern Ocean but illegal fishing still happens. Previous development of the areas and exploitation led to seals being almost wiped out in the South Falklands and whales in the Atlantic decreasing massively. No limits were set on development, so the area was exploited unsustainably. These only stopped due to bans in the 1960s on sealing and 1970s on whaling. However, they are still continued by some countries such as Russia, Norway and Japan — as they say, for scientific research. c

Tourism in Antarctica has also grown and become a concern for sustainability. Tourist numbers are limited and access to fragile sites is restricted. All waste has to be taken away and everyone is informed of the Antarctic Treaty to ensure that it is kept as a scientific area and preserved. All these areas show that development can be sustainable and the needs of the future can be preserved. d

Tourism in Antarctica has seen a significant increase in recent years with approximately 30,000 arrivals per year. Most visitors arrive by boat and are taken ashore in limited numbers. It is an expensive destination, very little litter/waste is left and research suggests that tourists do not affect the seals and penguins. Of the landing sites, 95% are not damaged. However, marine pollution from tourist and other sources is a threat, for instance the sinking of the *M/S Explorer* off the south Shetland Islands in 2007. IAATO guidelines are designed to manage impacts of tourism. However, membership of IAATO is not compulsory and so the Antarctic and Southern Ocean Coalition (ASOC) suggests limiting the total number of tourists and their method of arrival, with no land-based development and no air travel allowed, for example. e

Pollution by tourists, the fishing industry and scientific communities potentially affects the sustainability of the Antarctic environment. Discarded plastic, fishing nets and hooks, organic waste and sewage all contribute to environmental degradation. f

When evaluating the sustainability of tourism within Antarctica, there is a need for caution due to the fragility of the Antarctic environment. Impact studies by the Scott Polar Research Institute show that the impact of tourism is largely positive, with excellent educational provision on board ships that are visiting. Tourism perhaps offers the best hope for sustainability of the more recent developments, although in a globalising world tourist pressures are likely to increase. g

Taken as a whole, recent developments within Antarctica and the seas around it are more sustainable, as advances in technology and awareness for the environment increase. Rules of governance, such as the Madrid Protocol and Antarctic Treaty, prevent mining and ensure the sustainability of fragile areas. However, if unregulated, activities such as tourism and fishing can become unsustainable. h

e **15/20 marks awarded.** This is a somewhat erratic answer, which is good in parts, but repetitive and weak in others. The answer begins with an introduction that is a weakness, as the examiner cannot be sure at the outset that the student has engaged with the question. a Nevertheless a sustainability issue is introduced — whaling and fishing — albeit with some debatable facts. b The second paragraph continues with the theme, and the conceptual value is greater here, with a link to food webs and chains. c The third paragraph repeats several of the previous points. d Student B then moves to the theme of tourism, and the issue of sustainability is addressed more head on. e More detail is provided here, though the sense of evaluation required by the question is more implicit than explicit. f This is followed by a short paragraph, which perhaps could have been left until later. g The theme of tourism then returns, with a clear sense of evaluation. h A conclusion then follows, clearly linked to the question. Perhaps if a little more thought had gone into the structure of the answer beforehand, the overall mark would have been higher. High Level 3 awarded.

Set of questions B

Question 1

Describe the physical geography of Antarctica. (4 marks)

ⓔ **Mark scheme: 1 mark per valid point.**

> **Student A**
>
> Antarctica is 14 million km^2 in size **a**, and 98% of its surface area consists of ice that averages 2 km in thickness. **b** In terms of climate, it is a cold desert with an annual precipitation of only 200 mm along the coast, **c** and with lower totals inland. Around the coasts, temperatures are generally close to freezing in the summer months, or even slightly positive in the northern part of the Antarctic Peninsula. **d** During winter, monthly mean temperatures at coastal stations are between –10°C and –30°C, but temperatures may briefly rise towards freezing when winter storms bring warm air towards the Antarctic coast. **e**

ⓔ **4/4 marks awarded. a–e** Student A provides several valid descriptive statements.

> **Student B**
>
> Antarctica, the southernmost continent and site of the South Pole, is a virtually uninhabited, ice-covered land mass. **a** Most cruises to the continent visit the Antarctic Peninsula, which stretches toward South America. The cold continent's isolated landscape shelters rich wildlife, including many penguins. **b**

ⓔ **1/4 marks awarded. a b** It is difficult to find any statement of A-level quality, but perhaps 1 mark could be awarded for two weak descriptions.

Question 2

Table 2 shows information relating to internet usage around the world by region. Interpret the information shown. (6 marks)

Table 2 World internet usage by region (2014)

World region	Population (millions)	% of population with access to the internet	Growth of internet usage 2000–14 (%)	Proportion of world users of the internet (%)
Africa	1,136	26.5	6,499	9.8
Asia	4,096	34.7	1,113	45.7
Europe	741	70.5	454	19.2
Middle East	255	48.3	3,304	3.7
North America	353	87.7	187	10.2
Latin America	618	52.3	1,673	10.5
Oceania	39	72.9	252	0.9
World	7,238	42.3	741	100

Source: www.internetworldstats.com/stats.htm

ⓔ Mark scheme:

- Level 2 (4–6 marks): clear interpretation of the data in the table with some qualification and/or quantification that makes appropriate use of data to support. Interpretation may have some detail and/or sophistication.
- Level 1 (1–3 marks): basic interpretation of the data in the table (likely to be largely highs and lows), with limited use of data to support.

Student A

The table shows that the highest percentage of people with access to the internet is in North America at 87.7% and the lowest is in Africa at 26.5%. **ⓐ** This is to be expected, as North America is a developed continent where people have more income and can therefore buy computers, whereas Africa is the poorest continent. **ⓑ** Other high internet access areas are Europe and Oceania, again areas with high-income people.

The growth of the internet has been largest in Africa and Asia (and the Middle East). **ⓒ** This is obviously from a low base as the initial numbers in the year 2000 would have been low so the percentage increase looks large. **ⓓ** The opposite of this is in Europe and North America, as the people with access to the internet in 2000 would have been high.

The highest proportion of people who use the internet in the world is in Asia. **ⓔ** This is because the population of Asia is huge at four-sevenths of the world's population. Because there are so many people there, there are bound to be a high proportion of the world's people using the internet here. **ⓕ** It is obvious. Similarly, Oceania has the smallest number of people in the world and therefore the lowest proportion of world users.

ⓔ 3/6 marks awarded. ⓐ ⓒ ⓔ Student A provides a number of basic descriptions of the information in the data, **ⓑ ⓓ ⓕ** together with some simple statements of interpretation of these changes. Student A has not attempted to make any links within the data or made any sophisticated interpretation of them. Maximum Level 1 awarded.

Student B

The data shown in the table illustrate well how statistics need to be carefully interpreted. In the second column you have data that suggest that the developed world of North America and Europe is where the bulk of internet users are (but this is just a percentage of those with access to the web), whereas the final column suggests that the sheer numbers of internet users are in fact greatest in Asia (almost 46% of world users), especially when the population numbers are considered — we are looking at over 1 billion users here. **ⓐ** This latter fact illustrates that there has been a lot of outsourcing of ICT tasks to the countries of Asia by TNCs, some of which is undertaken in people's homes within the continent. **ⓑ** Another interesting comparison is that the proportion of internet users in the world is almost identical for North America and Africa. However, almost 90% of North Americans already have access to the web, whereas the potential for future growth is in Africa, where only about a quarter have access to the internet. c Africa could therefore offer a great deal of potential for internet providers. It is already the case that in Africa many people in rural areas use smart phones for their personal finances (using apps such as M-Pesa), much more than in areas such as Europe, for example. d

The world average for access to the internet is 42%, with the developing world of Africa and Asia being below that. The Middle East is not far above it though, and this seems to have had a huge increase in access, over 3,000% in fact, since 2000. e This could be due to the political turmoil that has occurred here in recent years that has been labelled the Arab Spring. f More and more young adults have shown their discontent with the regimes in their countries and this could be mirrored, or even facilitated by, the use of smart phones using various forms of social media. g It seems this is another area where the use of the internet could increase in the future.

e **6/6 marks awarded.** a Student B begins with an intelligent overview of the data, recognising their complexity. c e f This is then followed by a series of descriptive points that are both quantitative and qualitative, many of which are accompanied by sophisticated statements (interpretations), b d g, which link the data to the real world and aspects of geographical study within the global systems framework. This is an excellent answer, bearing in mind there are only 10 minutes to answer this question. Maximum marks awarded.

Question 3

Figure 4 provides information about gross domestic product (GDP) growth in the world between 2000 and 2015, and the varying contributions to that growth by different countries and regions. Using Figure 4 and your own knowledge, assess the relative contributions to global GDP growth.

(6 marks)

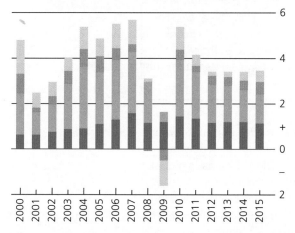

■ China   ■ Other emerging markets   ■ USA   ▪ Other rich countries

Souce: *The Economist*

Figure 4 Total world GDP growth and contributions by countries/regions (%) 2000–2015

ⓔ Mark scheme:

■ Level 2 (4–6 marks):

  ☐ AO1: demonstrates clear knowledge and understanding of concepts, processes, interactions and change.

  ☐ AO2: applies knowledge and understanding to the novel situation, offering clear analysis and assessment drawn appropriately from the context provided. Clear statement of relative contribution.

■ Level 1 (1–3 marks):

  ☐ AO1: demonstrates basic knowledge and understanding of concepts, processes, interactions, change.

  ☐ AO2: applies limited knowledge and understanding to the novel situation offering basic analysis and assessment drawn from the context provided. Tentative or no statement of relative contribution.

Student A

Figure 4 shows that between 2000 and 2015 there have been fluctuations in the overall rate of growth of GDP within the world. Throughout that period the growth has been positive except during 2009 where there was a global economic recession. **a** However, this only seems to have affected Western countries, as GDP growth remained positive in China and the other emerging markets such as India. Indeed, China has had positive GDP growth all through the period, contributing up to one-fifth of global GDP growth consistently — in 2009 it accounted for nearly all global growth. **b** Its most recent contribution is about 25% of global GDP growth. **c**

China's contribution to global GDP growth has consistently been larger than that of the USA, and for most of the period larger than all the other rich countries (such as Germany, France and the UK) combined. **d** The latter group of countries had a large drop in GDP in 2009 — as great as China's growth. However, for some of the time period the collective growth of countries such as India, Brazil and Russia (the other BRICs) has been greater than that of China, accounting for half of GDP growth in 2008, 2010 and 2011, for example. **e** This can be expected, as we are dealing with a group of countries here. However, in the most recent years, it appears that China has almost matched the GDP growth of these nations. It is clear that China and the other emerging nations now account for the largest proportion of GDP growth in the world. **f**

ⓔ 6/6 marks awarded. a Student A begins by making an overall comment, which is not required by the question. However, it does set the scene for the answer that follows. **b–d** A detailed account of the relative contribution of China to global levels of GDP growth is then provided, with several good comments being made. **e** This is followed by further description of relative contributions made by other emerging countries. **f** The answer concludes by joining these two areas (China and other emerging economies) together. The theme of relative contribution is central to the answer, underpinned by clear knowledge of the global economy. Maximum Level 2 awarded.

Student B

Figure 4 shows that China has increased its contribution of global GDP growth from about one-tenth in 2000 to about a third in 2015. The proportion has varied, with it reaching a peak in 2009 when it contributed about 80% of the growth, while much of the rest of the world was in recession. ⓐ Other emerging economies, such as India, Russia and Brazil, have also made major contributions to global GDP growth, reaching about 60% of the growth in the middle of the time period, between 2004 and 2010 (but not 2009). The USA has made a small contribution throughout the time period to global GDP growth, its largest proportion being in 2000. In 2008 and 2009 it actually decreased its contribution. Other rich countries have made varying contributions to global GDP growth, again reaching a peak in 2000, with significant periods being 2006, 2007 and 2010. Like the USA, they also had negative GDP growth in 2009, during the world recession. ⓑ Their decline was equal to China's growth.

ⓔ **3/6 marks awarded.** This answer is a bit of a cursory description of the data, which although accurate in terms of relative contributions, lacks clear and sophisticated assessment. ⓐ ⓑ The only areas where the student places the description of the data in a context are the links to the global recession. High Level 1 awarded.

Question 4

Assess the extent to which TNCs are both a cause and consequence of globalisation. (20 marks)

ⓔ **Mark scheme: see the generic extended-response mark scheme in the table on pages 48–49.**

Student A

Transnational corporations (TNCs) are large companies that produce or source goods and services internationally and market them worldwide. Many TNCs, such as McDonald's, Coca-Cola and Nestlé, are household names. TNCs are the major players in the global economy: the top 500 account for 70% of world trade and generate a large proportion of all foreign direct investment (FDI). They have enormous economic power and have been the driving force behind globalisation in recent decades. It could also be argued that by outsourcing and offshoring, companies inevitably become even more transnational, with mergers and acquisitions of foreign companies automatically leading to the creation of even larger TNCs. So, are TNCs also the outcome of globalisation? ⓐ

Global inequalities in human welfare are closely linked to economic development, which in turn is strongly influenced by FDI decisions taken by TNCs. Where economic development has made least progress (e.g. in sub-Saharan Africa) it is hardly surprising that infant mortality rates are high and life expectancy is low. ⓑ Africa, the poorest continent, has 15% of the world's population yet attracts less than 3% of global FDI. Deterred by poor economic and social infrastructures, political instability and corruption, investment opportunities in much of sub-Saharan Africa remain unattractive to TNCs. Hence, globalisation of large parts of this continent is being manipulated by investment, or rather the lack of it, by TNCs. ⓒ

It is often argued that TNCs locate manufacturing plants in developing countries in order to exploit weak labour and pollution laws. The US–Mexico border region has experienced massive economic growth since the 1980s, due largely to investment on the Mexican side of the border by US, European and Asian TNCs. This investment mainly comprises branch plants or maquiladoras, which manufacture a wide range of goods including clothes, chemicals and electronics, and then export them across the border to the USA. d

The main attractions of the border region are low labour costs and proximity to US markets. Another main factor here has been the creation of the North American Free Trade Association (NAFTA), a major example of free trade between nations. e The promotion of free trade, encouraged by national governments and the World Trade Organization (WTO), facilitates corporate global production lines and this sort of TNC activity. Deregulation of capital markets has also allowed profits to be moved from place to place and so results in increased TNC activity. f

The most publicised aspects of globalisation have been offshoring and outsourcing. In practice, most offshoring means transferring production from developed countries to developing countries where labour and other costs are lower and access to foreign markets is easier. Outsourcing involves subcontracting production to another company, which provides goods and services sold under the TNC brand. Through offshoring and outsourcing, TNCs from developed countries have in effect created more home-grown TNCs in order to undertake the work. For example, companies such as Apple and Primark subcontract the work out to other companies who may in turn operate across regions such as Southeast Asia — they are growing as a consequence of globalisation. g These have often been accused of creating 'sweatshop' employment, characterised by low wages, child labour and poor working conditions.

In contrast there are advantages created by TNCs, such as the creation and growth of employment, which in turn raises the GNP of the host country. TNCs have also resulted in the growth of global production lines and increased trade in a globalised world, largely through containerisation. These TNCs, such as Apple and Samsung, are driving the globalisation of transport systems. h

In conclusion, the role of TNCs within the global economy is highly significant. The importance of TNCs as drivers of globalisation cannot be overstated. They have had an impact on rapid industrialisation in emerging economies such as China, India and Mexico. It is also clear that they themselves have increased in size, number and influence in recent years, so indeed it could be argued they are both a cause and a consequence of globalisation. i

e **20/20 marks awarded.** The answer starts with a solid introduction that defines, and exemplifies, TNCs and also engages with one of the themes of the question: cause. a This is followed by a brief statement that connects with the second theme: consequences. b The next paragraph, which initially appears to be not related to the question, by introducing some connections to other aspects of the subject, is cleverly brought back to 'cause' in c, the final sentence. d e The next sections again connect with the theme of 'cause' and although not explicitly linked to it, they nevertheless provide a good case study of the spread of globalisation as a result of TNC expansion. [f] This is then supported by a sophisticated point regarding the importance of free trade. [g] The next paragraph demonstrates thorough knowledge and understanding of the operations of TNCs in the twenty-first century — offshoring and outsourcing — and uses this knowledge to discuss how TNCs are being further developed. This is a very strong paragraph with a coherent sense of assessment. [h] The next paragraph is not as strong but is continuing to explain how TNCs are driving globalisation through transport systems. [i] The conclusion is explicitly aimed at the 'extent to which' part of the task. All elements of the mark scheme for Level 4 have been addressed. Maximum marks awarded.

Student B

TNCs are companies that operate and sell products in a number of different countries across the globe. For example, a very well known TNC is Walmart, which operates across 13 countries and employs over 900,000 people indirectly and directly. Incentives of TNCs are mainly profit based and they aim to keep their costs of production to a minimum. [a]

Since the 1960s TNCs have been responsible for increasing globalisation throughout the world. This was due to TNCs relocating their manufacturing and production factories overseas, mainly to the Far East (South Korea, Hong Kong, Taiwan). In doing this, TNCs contributed to the growth of the world's economy by introducing trade and new methods of business to previously undeveloped countries. In recent years TNCs have moved away from the countries listed before (also known as the Asian Tigers — first-generation NICs) and moved towards China and India for their manufacturing. [b]

For example, Apple has manufacturing plants in China and Malaysia already, and last year developed a cheaper version of the iPhone aimed at markets such as China and India, where income isn't high enough. This was designed to be affordable while still having the status and branding of luxury Apple goods. This is an example of a TNC perpetuating globalisation. [c]

As TNCs progress through poor countries looking for cheap costs of production they provide many positive impacts. For the host country the relocation of production provides a source of reliable employment. Increased employment leads to a positive multiplier effect in the country. As incomes increase so too does consumption, boosting the country's economy. Local ancillary firms are required to service the factories, for example, caterers and cleaners. This again stimulates the growth of local businesses and contributes towards a growing economy. However, the economic impacts can also be negative; over-reliance by the host country on the TNC as a source of revenue can be very bad. When the TNC decides to relocate in order to keep costs down it can leave the local economy in a very poor state. It can also leave a high rate of structural employment and cause quality of life in the country to fall again. [d]

However, there can be many positive social factors to the host country also, for example, the increased quality of life and improved living standards can mean many people now live above the poverty line. Stable wages mean that people can buy more food, leading to much lower levels of malnutrition. As well as this, TNCs train staff in how to use technology and improve their skills. This transfer of technology can mean a more skilled and educated workforce. This can lead to the growth of local businesses and eventually some TNCs originating in the country. ⓔ An example of this is the first TNC to be started in South Korea, Samsung, which now sells its products on a global scale. Another example is Huawei technologies, which originated in China. Although not as established as Samsung, Huawei is much newer to the market and is pioneering the development of technology used in the government secret service. ⓕ These are examples of TNCs being a consequence of globalisation.

In conclusion, TNCs have impacted the global economy very positively in the past few years. China, for example, has benefited very much from the huge amounts of FDI injected into the country's economy. I believe this to be evidence enough for the benefits of TNCs on the global economy and hence a major cause. Over-reliance can be very harmful to a country's economy and in order to combat this, the home government often encourages growth of domestic businesses as well as encouraging investment from TNCs, therefore creating home-grown TNCs. ⓖ

ⓔ **10/20 marks awarded.** ⓐ Student B also begins by defining and exemplifying TNCs. ⓑ The next paragraph then gives a chronological account of the growth of TNCs that implicitly addresses the 'cause' theme of the question. ⓒ The next paragraph provides good support for the theme of 'cause'. ⓓ The following paragraph lacks focus on the task, and discusses impacts of the growth of TNCs in a country. This is not made relevant. ⓔ This irrelevance appears to continue in the next paragraph, but eventually the student manages to bring in the theme of 'consequence'. ⓕ This point is then supported well by the examples of Samsung and Huawei. ⓖ The conclusion lacks clarity and is tentative in addressing the 'extent to which' element. Level 2 criteria have been met with some sense of assessment, and, bearing in mind the exemplification used, it merits the top mark within the level.

Changing places
Question 1

Distinguish between outsider and insider perspectives of a place. (4 marks)

ⓔ **Mark scheme: 1 mark per valid point.**

Student A

Outsider perspectives are the views of a person who does not live in a community. ⓐ Their view is often a personal view of entering a locale or landscape and learning how people live and feel about a place. ⓑ On the other hand, insider perspectives refer to the development of a sense of place through everyday experiences in familiar settings. ⓒ Daily rhythms of life and life experiences underpin the subjectivity that is the basis for developing a sense of place of the community. ⓓ

ⓔ **4/4 marks awarded.** ⓐ–ⓓ Student A provides four valid points.

Student B

Insider people have a strong relationship with the places they are familiar with. This is the main reason why people living within a place are more likely to oppose developments within their local area than those from outside. a This 'nimbyism' can be seen with local opposition to housing developments, wind farms and fracking proposals. b Increasingly, however, many people feel like outsiders in a society. Graffiti on historic buildings or litter in an area of outstanding beauty are examples of this. c

e **3/4 marks awarded.** a–c Student B provides three valid points.

Question 2

Table 3 shows census data for two places within London — Shadwell and Hampstead Garden Suburb. Interpret the contrasts shown in Table 3.　　　(6 marks)

Table 3 Census data for two London districts (2011)

Census criteria (2011)	Population density per ha.	Population under 17 years of age (%)	Population aged 17–64 (%)	Population aged 65 and over (%)	% of households with an average of more than one person per room	Outright ownership of housing (%)	Households with two or more cars/vans (%)
Shadwell	399	31.8	64.3	3.9	24.5	3.6	3.8
Hampstead Garden Suburb	11.9	23.9	57.1	19.0	0.6	48.4	57.8

Source: ONS

e Mark scheme:
- Level 2 (4–6 marks): clear interpretation of the contrasts in the data in the table with some qualification and/or quantification that makes appropriate use of data to support. Interpretation may have some detail and/or sophistication.
- Level 1 (1–3 marks): basic interpretation of the contrasts in the data in the table (likely to be largely highs and lows), with limited use of data to support.

Student A

There is a clear difference in the population as the percentage of over 65-year-olds in Hampstead Garden Suburb (HGS) is almost five times higher than that of Shadwell. a This will mean that there will be greater provision for the elderly in this area with probably a relatively large amount of care homes and similar residential homes. It will also mean that services such as mobile visiting nurses and meals on wheels will be more common. b

In terms of overcrowding, there is a significantly greater problem in Shadwell, with nearly a quarter of the households having an average of more than one person per room when only 0.6% of the households in HGS have this issue. **c** This is symptomatic of the fact that the houses will be much larger in HGS, possibly old Victorian properties, and in Shadwell there will be more small terraced houses housing larger families. **d** This is supported by the huge difference in population density — closely packed terraced houses in Shadwell and large houses with big gardens in HGS. A garden suburb indeed.

Finally, HGS has much higher car ownership and home ownership. **e** All this points to HGS being a wealthy area, with many wealthy, retired people living in large houses and having two or more cars, and a large proportion of low-income residents, possibly students or immigrants, living in Shadwell. **f**

e **6/6 marks awarded.** Student A has provided **a** **c** **e** three detailed descriptions of the differences shown with **b** **d** **f** linked interpretation of these differences. Maximum marks awarded.

Student B

Shadwell is a poor, densely populated area **a**, with not many old people living there. This is shown by the high population density (399 per ha.), the low house and car ownership (less than 4% each) and a similar percentage being over 65 years old. **b**

On the other hand, Hampstead Garden Suburb is a wealthy, sparsely populated area, **c** with a lot of old people living there. This is shown by low population density (11.9 per ha.), the high rates of ownership of houses and two or more cars (nearly 50% and 58% respectively) and almost 20% being over 65. **d**

Of the two, I would prefer to live in Hampstead Garden Suburb because it is likely to have more green space between the houses and there are still almost a quarter of the population under 17, so there will still be a nightlife. **e**

e **3/6 marks awarded.** **b** **d** There are several statements of description of differences, with the student taking a simple route through the data, largely in two separate accounts. It is not good A-level technique to describe contrasts in data in such a straightforward manner. **a** **c** **e** The interpretation is also weak. Maximum Level 1 awarded.

Question 3

Figures 5 and 6 provide information about the representation of the Lake District and the town of Keswick. Using Figures 5 and 6 and your own knowledge, evaluate the ways in which these places have been represented.

(6 marks)

The Lake District has been rebranded several times in the past. Until about 300 years ago it was viewed as barren and wild. It was not until the eighteenth century that natural landscapes were seen as something to be admired. Attitudes towards the Lake District began to change after 1750, when a number of influential travel guidebooks reframed the landscape as picturesque (like a painting) and sublime (awe-inspiring and wonderful). Thomas West's *Guide to the Lakes* (1778) described the rocky scenery in Borrowdale as 'sublimely terrible' and likely to inspire 'reverential awe'. Such comments encouraged visitors to the area, although most admired the scenery from the valley floor, rather than venturing onto the hills.

A further rebranding occurred in 1951, when the area was designated a National Park. In 2012 the Lake District sought, but failed, to gain World Heritage status, although another bid is to be submitted in 2016. In the current rebranding plans, the Lake District, and especially the town of Keswick (see Figure 6), is keen to become recognised as the Adventure Capital of the UK.

Figure 5 The Lake District, including Keswick

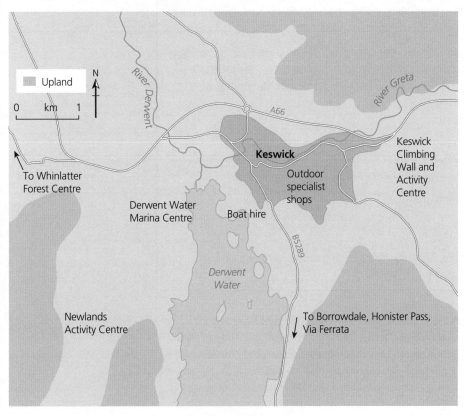

Figure 6 Keswick as an adventure holiday hub

ⓔ Mark scheme:

■ Level 2 (4–6 marks):
   ☐ AO1: demonstrates clear knowledge and understanding of concepts, processes, interactions and change.
   ☐ AO2: applies knowledge and understanding to the novel situation, offering clear analysis and evaluation drawn appropriately from the context provided.
■ Level 1 (1–3 marks):
   ☐ AO1: demonstrates basic knowledge and understanding of concepts, processes, interactions and change.
   ☐ AO2: applies limited knowledge and understanding to the novel situation, offering basic analysis and evaluation drawn from the context provided.

Student A

Figures 5 and 6 illustrate various ways in which the Lake District and the town of Keswick have been represented in the past in books, and more recently on a map. In all cases they are seeking to capitalise on the region's outstanding natural resources, the landscape and considerable experience in outdoor recreational provision. ⓐ Such representation of the area has been important for almost 300 years as guidebooks such as that of Thomas West's in 1778 testify. The emotive words used in Figure 5 — 'picturesque', 'sublime' and 'reverential' — all support this view. ⓑ

When designation as a National Park took place in 1951, the main purpose was to generate tourist revenue, both directly through employment, for example in outdoor adventure centres, and indirectly, for example when farmers supply local food to hotels and restaurants.

All of the above and the failed attempt to become a World Heritage area strived to engender a greater appreciation for, and interest in, conserving the landscape. ⓒ They also provide facilities that locals as well as visitors can use, thus enriching community life for all people in the area.

The facilities shown in the map of Keswick, Figure 6, all with a view to creating an adventure holiday hub, also fit in with the need to encourage health-related fitness, an important government initiative. ⓓ

So, a variety of forms of representation have been used, and they all have adventure and exercise as common themes. ⓔ

ⓔ **6/6 marks awarded.** Student A has engaged with the theme of evaluation throughout. References are clearly made to the stimulus material, but then in most cases the student makes commentary on how these materials support the idea of representation. ⓐ–ⓓ Some examples of such commentary are indicated. ⓔ The answer ends with a neat conclusion. This is an excellent answer. Maximum Level 2 awarded.

Student B

In the 1700s, the Lake District was rebranded as a place to be admired by visitors, and a number of guidebooks were written to encourage people to visit the area. **a** These books used words that compared the landscape with a painting, and also made some of the area seem frightening or scary — equally enticing for some adventurous people. **b**

This move to encourage visitors has continued to the present day, in which the area and the town of Keswick in particular have been advertised as an adventure holiday hub. **c** So, a constant theme of the representation has been to make the area important for tourism and to encourage people to come and explore it, and have fun at the same time. **d** Today, you can go to Keswick and take part in outdoor activities such as walking, boating and climbing on a wall, and you can also visit an activity centre. Adventure holidays are therefore important in the marketing of the area and the town. **e**

e **4/6 marks awarded.** Although this is a much more straightforward answer, Student B engages with the stimulus material and **a c** not only demonstrates an understanding of what it is saying about the region, but also **b d e** shows some evidence of evaluation. It is a pity that some of the ideas were not developed further. Low Level 2 awarded.

Question 4

Evaluate how past and present connections have shaped the characteristics of one place you have studied.
(20 marks)

e **Mark scheme: see the generic extended-response mark scheme in the table on pages 48–49.**

Student A

Saltaire is a model industrial village and textile mill north of Bradford, built by the industrialist Sir Titus Salt. The village on the edge of Shipley is a perfectly preserved 25-acre site of one man's utopia. Having built his fortune on the use of alpaca and mohair, Salt found that by the late 1840s his factory in the centre of Bradford was too small to meet the demands of his new textiles. However, in 1849 a major cholera epidemic struck Bradford. Being a strict congregational Christian, Salt stated that 'cholera was God's voice to the people', and so he decided to build a better community for his workers. **a**

Saltaire was built between 1852 and 1872 and was modelled on the buildings of the Italian Renaissance period, a period (in Salt's opinion) when both cultural and social advancement took place. Salt's mill emulated an Italian Palazzo, was larger than St Paul's Cathedral and was the largest factory in the world when it opened. It was surrounded by a school, a hospital, a railway station, parks, baths, wash houses, 45 alms houses and 850 houses. The style and size of each house reflected the place of the head of the family in the factory hierarchy.

Twenty-two streets were created, and all but two (Victoria and Albert Streets) were named after members of Salt's family. The church was the first public building to be completed, and there was not a single public house. b

Saltaire today remains almost as Salt built it. The houses, streets and integral public buildings are protected by law as Grade 1 listed properties. The village's current characteristics therefore are a strong reflection of the past. All that has happened is that the internal aspects of the buildings have been modernised or in some cases changed in purpose from their original function. For example, the huge Salt's mill has been converted into a number of uses. c Part of it is used to make satellite TV equipment (Sky+ boxes), which are sold all over the UK, a connection of today. Other parts of the mill house shops and cafés, and some floors are used to display the work of the painter David Hockney, which people from all over the world travel to see. He is an artist born in Yorkshire, so it makes sense to see his work in his home county. So, it is clear that a place built by a strong past connection is having its current characteristics shaped by current connections.

e 13/20 marks awarded. The place selected, Saltaire, is described well and in detail. a The historical reasons (past connections) for its development are well explained, and b the clear description of its characteristics both in the past and in the present is equally strong. c The third paragraph covers aspects of the present, indicating the degree to which the present has, or has not, resulted in change to the characteristics of Saltaire. Several aspects of Level 3 are being addressed here. The major weakness is that the student has not developed a sense of 'links' or 'connections' sufficiently strongly. There could have been more analysis and evaluation of the flows of people, resources, money and investment into the place. Mid-Level 3 awarded.

Student B

Trafalgar Square is known throughout the world as a place of coming together and meeting other people. It lies on the north bank of the river Thames, about 500 m from the river itself and on a marked slope from north to south. This slope marks the first level of river terraces that have been produced over thousands of years by the river in this part of the Thames valley — a strong past connection in the physical geography sense. a

Trafalgar Square was the first deliberately planned public square in London. It evolved in stages between 1830 and 1860, and was the capital's first attempt at a grand historical monument commemorating military victory and embodying national pride. Hence it was always designed to bring people together from all parts of the country. The space to the south of the square, on the lower level of the slope, was known as Charing Cross, itself a small open space. This area had previously served as a place of public meetings, proclamations, pillory and execution. People travelled from all over the city to witness public executions and people being punished publicly.

The upper part of the slope was originally occupied by the King's Mews, a large area of stables. In front of the Mews were various taverns, shops and houses. The demolition of the mews and the nearby buildings began with the project to build a national art gallery. This work began in 1832, sited to the north of the space, and exactly where the mews had been. A terrace was also constructed on the same level as the gallery, with a series of stone steps descending to the square itself. These steps are still there today. The gallery was completed in 1838, the same year in which Nelson's monument was commissioned. This is a 150 ft granite column with its crowning statue, which was not completed until 1859.

So already by the middle of the nineteenth century, Trafalgar Square had come to make a name for itself both in the country and beyond. People came to see the splendid constructions, the famous column and the paintings that were beginning to be housed in the gallery. Its characteristics were being shaped by its historical connections.

Further changes were to come. In 1874, a new road to the riverside was created — Northumberland Avenue, named after the large Jacobean house that used to stand on the corner of the square. The final part of Trafalgar Square as we know it came in 1910 with the building of Admiralty Arch as a grand gateway to the Mall. Also by this time two large fountains had been designed by Lutyens and placed between Nelson's Column and the National Gallery. These added to the attractions of the site, and tourists from all over the world were being attracted to it. Today, New Year revellers like to soak themselves in the fountains. b

Today, Trafalgar Square is a landmark in central London enjoyed by Londoners and all visitors alike. It is a lively place, which is often used for a wide range of activities, including special events and celebrations, St Patrick's Day, Pride events, Eid and Chinese New Year, and rallies and demonstrations. All of these events bring people together and ensure that its central characteristic, that of being a large meeting space, is maintained. Trafalgar Square is one place that all visitors to London make sure they visit.

Trafalgar Square began its existence as a public meeting place for the people of London. It has now evolved into a meeting place for people across the UK to show their pleasure, as in the case of London being awarded the Olympic Games, or to show their displeasure, as when it was a focal point during the CND protests against nuclear warfare and the poll tax in the 1980s. c Its characteristics certainly have been shaped by its past and present connections.

e 20/20 marks awarded. It is difficult to find fault with this answer. The sense of place is strong; the detail provided, both historical and contemporary, is relevant and accurate. Student B has also appreciated the nature of the task — the need to link connections with characteristics — and his/her focus in addressing the task is first-rate. a–c There are also a number of places where the student makes connections (links) to other aspects of geography, including physical processes, tourism and conflict. A strong, detailed and coherent analysis has been made. All Level 4 criteria have been addressed. High Level 4 awarded.

Knowledge check answers

Knowledge check answers

1 The 'shrinking world' can be illustrated by:
- Up to the mid-nineteenth century most travel was on horseback, with an average speed of 10 mph.
- Steam trains then moved at up to 70 mph, and steam ships at over 30 mph.
- By the mid-twentieth century, air travel was much more common, again reducing travel times across the world.
- From the late twentieth century, communication has become almost instant with the internet.

2 The MINT countries are Mexico, Indonesia, Nigeria and Turkey.

3 At the highest level, the top of the service hierarchy is to be found in world cities such as London, New York and Tokyo, which are the major nuclei of global industrial and financial command functions. Other cities of prominence include Frankfurt, Chicago, Paris, Milan and Los Angeles.

4 'Just-in-time' production is a system designed to minimise the costs of holding stocks of raw materials and components by carefully planned scheduling and flow of these materials and components through the production process. It requires a very efficient ordering system and reliability of delivery. It has given rise to a new term in the transportation of goods: logistics.

5 India has become one of the most attractive locations for the outsourcing of services, and in particular, the state of Karnataka, which houses Bangalore — often known as India's 'Silicon City'. Much of this outsourcing has involved call centre work and software development. Labour costs are much lower, but the workforce is both highly educated and has good use of the English language. India is the second-largest English-speaking human resource in the world and has the world's third-largest 'brain bank', with around 2.5 million technical professionals. There is also a burgeoning 'middle class' of some 250–350 million people with increasing purchasing power.

6 For:
- A huge potential market of around 500 million people.
- The combined strength of the members form a powerful trade bloc.
- Freedom of movement for workers within a wide employment market.

Against:
- Poor distribution of EU income, particularly as the Common Agricultural Policy (CAP) takes so much of the budget.
- Over-bureaucracy within the European Commission has brought into question its efficiency.
- The adoption of some European laws has been inconsistent across the Union.

7 For example, in India, Ujjivan Financial Services was established in 2005. The company now has 2.3 million customers, operates in 22 states and is one of the most dominant organisations in Indian microfinancing. Its high loan repayment rate of 99.9% is critical to its success. The scheme uses group lending so that it becomes the collective responsibility of the individuals. As they may all want access to future loans, there is increased awareness that no one individual should default on the loan.

8 An imaginary example of a hub company would be a US-owned TNC that outsources some manufacturing to a South Korean TNC, which in turn has a branch factory in China. The US company also has a branch factory in Mexico and a subsidiary in Germany. In addition, much of the administrative support for all of these is undertaken in back-office work in India. There is therefore a complex web of interconnections.

9 The main features of Article 1 of the UN Charter are as follows:
- To maintain international peace and security, and to that end, to take effective collective measures for the prevention and removal of threats to the peace, and for the suppression of acts of aggression or other breaches of the peace.
- To develop friendly relations among nations based on respect for the principle of equal rights and self-determination of peoples.
- To achieve international cooperation in solving international problems of an economic, social, cultural or humanitarian character, and in promoting and encouraging respect for human rights and for fundamental freedoms for all without distinction as to race, sex, language or religion.

10 NATO is a military alliance established in 1949. It was set up to organise collective defence when an external party attacked members from the North Atlantic area. At the time of establishment the main threat was from the Soviet Union (now Russia), but it has also launched military activity in the Balkans, Afghanistan and Libya. There are currently 28 members.

11 The UN plays an integral part in social and economic development through its UN Development Programme (UNDP). UNDP administers the UN Capital Development Fund, which helps developing countries grow their economies by supplementing existing sources of capital assistance by means of grants and loans. In addition, the World Health Organization (WHO), UNAIDS, the Global Fund to Fight AIDS, Tuberculosis and Malaria, the UN Population Fund, and the World Bank also play essential roles. The UN annually publishes the Human Development Index (HDI), which ranks countries in terms of poverty, literacy, education and life expectancy.

12 Ethical trade means that retailers, companies and their suppliers take responsibility for improving the working conditions of the people who make the products they sell. Most of these workers are employed by supplier companies around the world, many of them based in developing countries where laws designed to protect workers' rights are inadequate or not enforced. Companies with a commitment to ethical trade adopt a code of labour practice that they expect all their suppliers to work towards. Such a code addresses issues like wages, hours of work, health and safety, and the right to join free trade unions.

13 The Antarctic Convergence (AC) marks the location where surface waters of the Southern Ocean moving northward sink below sub-Antarctic waters. The AC is a region of faster water current speeds and strong horizontal gradients in density, temperature and salinity. The AC also marks the location of one of several strong atmospheric jets within the Antarctic Circumpolar Current (ACC), which flows eastward around Antarctica. The AC marks an important climatic boundary in terms of both air–sea fluxes, and the heat and salt budgets of the oceans.

14 Krill are small crustaceans and are found in all the world's oceans. Krill are considered an important trophic level connection — near the bottom of the food chain — because they feed on phytoplankton and zooplankton, converting these into a form suitable for many larger animals for whom krill make up the largest part of their diet. In the Southern Ocean, one species of krill makes up an estimated biomass of over 350 million tonnes. Of this, over half is eaten by whales, seals, penguins, squid and fish each year.

15 The International Whaling Commission (IWC) is the global body charged with the conservation of whales and the management of whaling. The IWC currently has 88 member governments from countries all over the world. All members are signatories to the International Convention for the Regulation of Whaling. The Commission coordinates and funds conservation work on many species of cetacean. The Commission has also adopted a strategic plan for whale-watching in order to facilitate the further development of this activity in a way that is responsible and consistent with international best practice.

16 Locale refers to a place as a setting for particular practices that mark it out from other places. As well as being a location, place has a physical landscape (buildings, parks, infrastructures of transport and communication, signs, memorials, etc.) and a social landscape (everyday practices of work, education and leisure, among others).

17 The phrase 'field of care' refers to what Tuan called the 'affective bond between people and place or setting'. Tuan argued that through experience of a place, the daily activity of living in and moving through specific environments, we come to form attachments to places — they become private places. They are the places where people create interpersonal ties and develop social capital, both of which require extended time spent there as well as material settings.

18 Some writers contend that the process of globalisation highlights, rather than eliminates, place, arguing that distinct differences in place are seen nowhere more clearly than through uneven economic and social development. Using any urban high street as a context, for example, place is not constituted by its own locality but by its global connections. On a high street you will see not only shops and offices that connect with the wider world through their ownership and the goods they sell, but also a range of ethnic groups among the people who walk on the pavements. Rather than the idea of a 'local community', a community is built through layered local–global interactions.

19 Location: a point in space with specific links to other points in space.

A sense of place: the subjective feelings associated with living in a place.

20 The varying identities of people involved in the European migration crisis of 2015/16 included:
- the migrants themselves, fleeing war and persecution. Perhaps there were economic migrants there too, seeking a better life.
- the aid workers handing out food, water and other essential items
- police and troops, seeking to maintain some sort of order
- media reporters and cameramen, informing the world of what was happening
- national politicians, trying to find a way to deal with the crisis; there were differing views among them
- people who lived miles away, wanting to help and pressurising governments
- people who lived miles away, wanting to 'send migrants back' and pressurising governments

21
- Rebranding: the process of regenerating a city's economy and physical fabric as well as projecting a new, positive urban image to the wider world.
- Re-imaging: the process of creating a new perspective of a place as seen by others, at home and abroad.
- Regeneration: a combination of physical, economic and social renewal of a city or part of a city.

Index

Note: **bold** page numbers indicate key terms.

Index